# REDEFINING TALENT MANAGEMENT

## HOW TO BUILD A TALENT POWERED ORGANISATION.

## DR. AMIT DAS

To

*All my bosses and students who made a difference in my professional career.*

*"Not only it is absolutely morally necessary to have a diverse workforce, but it is also crucial for business. Now is the perfect time for businesses to show their dedication to a brighter future by creating a workforce that is more diverse and egalitarian. The difficulties faced by business executives who want to hire a diverse workforce often appear virtually insurmountable. Having said that, business leaders made some audacious commitments to reaffirm and reenergise their commitment to equality, diversity, and inclusion in the workplace in order to contribute to the creation of a more fair organisation."*

*– Dr. Amit Das, Motivational Speaker, Leadership Coach and Mentor.*

# Contents

# Foreword

*"Nothing we do is more important than hiring and developing people. At the end of the day, you bet on people, not on strategies."- Lawrence Bossidy, Former COO of General Electric*

**Dear Reader,**

Thank you for taking the time to learn more about "Redefining Talent Management" to make a talent ready organisation. You are aware that having the best talent is necessary to succeed in the industry nowadays. This book, "Redefining Talent Management," is the most authoritative book on the market for locating and making use of the greatest people. This book has the most cutting-edge concepts and the most up-to-date methods, procedures, and tools to help you start a thorough talent management programme that will propel you and your staff to the top. This book outlines a complete, integrated set of talent strategies that are appropriate for the evolving workplace and that will significantly increase firms' effectiveness.

This book, "Redefining Talent Management," is the most comprehensive book of its kind, is now the go-to resource for HR professionals, CEOs, and business executives who want to take the lead in developing a diverse, skilled, and engaged workforce. You invest a lot of time, money, and other resources into developing that talent because you are aware of what it takes.

Your employees are the one thing that truly sets your company apart from the competition. Do you possess the correct ability at the right time and place? Having a "workforce" is no longer sufficient; you also need a high-impact talent force. The authors begin by outlining the significant social, cultural, and economic changes that are revolutionising hiring as we now know it. This book shows what they want and how to address those demands while expanding your business.

The book employs a 360-degree perspective to explain how each stakeholder perceives the components of talent management, what they require from each component, and the misunderstandings and conflicts that develop among the stakeholders and restrict the potential of individuals. The author provides managers, HR experts, senior executives, and leaders with useful guidance on how to collaborate to create a skilled and engaged team. The book discusses talent management topics like growth, coaching, feedback, remuneration, and performance. The book validates what effective people managers do and provides detailed advice for anyone looking to improve their talent management abilities.

Leadership must optimise alignment, competence, and engagement within their organisations more than ever before. Human resource planning and strategic talent management are used to convey and examine many aspects of global talent management to readers. Organisational executives and HR professionals who deal with talent management, today's most important business problem, must read this. This book offers a wealth of inspiring principles, methods, and models for formulating and putting into practise talent management strategies. This book's sections include cutting-edge methods, step-by-step useful management approaches, and informative resources that will enable you to find and nurture emerging talent; motivate; mentor; and prepare your future leaders.

You'll discover the significance of identifying talent demands as well as the variables that may have an impact on them. Additionally, you'll learn how to develop a HR management strategy that effectively addresses the needs you pinpoint. Most businesses recognise the value of having efficient recruiting and recruitment procedures. They are aware that they must choose and hire talented people if they are to succeed and stay competitive. Competitors that place a high value on hiring will highlight this lack of forethought when they secure the finest staff, giving them a competitive advantage. What could be more crucial than putting your attention on attracting, choosing, correctly segmenting, developing, and keeping top talent? Is talent present throughout your organisation?

*Do you know how to effectively assess raw human talent if talent is the key predictor of whether a firm is up or down, a success or a failure?*

Regardless of the organisation involved, the ideas offered with useful examples will assist in extending everyone's awareness so they can build and give the proper solutions that match their needs of strengthening the talent pipeline. The procedures at your organisation, however elegantly planned and well benchmarked, don't seem to translate into the depth of talent you actually require. To help every professional, company leader, and executive understand how to provide real business value by concentrating on talent, this book, "Redefining Talent Management," focuses on talent and succession management principles and practises.

Learn how applicants are using technology to assess new possibilities, benchmark salaries, and establish new backchannels for discussing work life. Make the most of these new technologies to expand your talent pool, access fresh sources of competitive intelligence, and maintain your lead over the competition. You will learn how world-class organisations like rely on their processes for developing leadership potential to achieve outstanding results decade after decade.

In the volatile environment of today, managers can't effectively predict their company's demands, let alone their talent needs. In this book, Dr. Amit Das takes a radical new look at the talent management issue. He introduces new concepts for making sure your organisation has the talent it needs when it needs them, drawing on cutting-edge talent supply chain management and several corporate examples. It is both practical and provocative.

> *"Many talent-management approaches and philosophies now in use in organisations are outmoded due to the fluid nature of employment. Even though there have been significant changes brought about by globalisation, technological advancements, automation, workforce diversification, the push for sustainable practises and the escalating pace of transformation and pandemic survival, a recent study found that the amount of time HR spends on tasks did not significantly improve their talent management skills. In this VUCA, ever changing business landscape, how people are hired, chosen, taught, allocated, developed, rewarded, and assessed no longer works according to what was once best practice."*

Talented people are in high demand. Organisations must wage a more intense recruitment battle for qualified workers as their reliance on specialists and experts grows. Identification, acquisition, development, and retention of talent for a company are all continuous processes that fall under the heading of talent management. This book provides a road map for engagement, talent development, and management excellence because it is structured around a cogent concept and is supported by credible evidence. These strategies assist middle managers in achieving the objectives of their business while enabling their staff to achieve their own. They may be used in a variety of challenging scenarios and organisational issues, as well as everyday motivation and inspiration.

Thank you for taking the time to read this book.

So, happy reading and learning to all my readers.

**Carpe diem.**

**Dr. Amit Das**

**Motivational Speaker, Leadership Coach, and Mentor.**

# Preface

*"The secret of my success is that we have gone to exceptional lengths to hire the best people in the world."*
*-Steve Jobs*

## *A talent pipeline is most effective when it's specific.*

Talent Management entails predicting human capital demand and maintaining a talent-ready organisation, developing a strategy to meet this need; and then putting the plan into action in the future. In this book, you will learn about the difficulties that talent management faces as well as the prerequisites for its success. This book outlines important considerations for developing, implementing, and integrating various strategic talent management processes, including hiring, performance management, pay, succession planning, and development. The book also explores how to persuade businesses to support, adopt, and sustain efficient strategic talent management procedures.

The global pandemic of 2020 taught us things that we would never have learned in business school, and we will never forget those teachings. Talent management, like other aspects of human resources, will need to be reevaluated and redefined in the post-pandemic future. Talent management and strategic workforce planning both include everything done to attract, keep, develop, reward, and motivate employees.

Today's top workers also have radically changed expectations for themselves and how they approach their jobs. Learn how to create and put into action a world-class talent plan that supports company goals and how to identify success measures. Talent is a precious and occasionally rare commodity, so talent management is becoming more and more crucial.

While mid-level managers are still expected to recruit, engage, keep, and develop talent, most organisations focus most of their development resources on the C-suite. However, managing daily responsibilities while maintaining team performance and navigating obstacles leaves little time for management planning. In the framework of talent management, I take into account that talent is defined from the perspective of the organisation's core values in connection to the mission-critical employees whose value-add directly aids the organisation in realising its fundamental values.

> *"Organisations must find, nurture, and keep brilliant people if they are to flourish. When talent is effectively managed, your department's success increases, which boosts your organisation's competitiveness."*

It may seem quite esoteric to consider the possibility of releasing someone else's potential by encouraging them and pushing them to greater heights. You are astounded at what can happen when the limitations that companies place on their own employees are eliminated when you witness the cumulative impact of everyone in a company functioning at their highest level and actually working together. The moment has come to reinvent talent management. In light of the difficult times we are now experiencing, it is more crucial than ever to hire and keep the best employees. Your "talent management" will inevitably leak if the job market is open. Additionally, growing competitiveness necessitates an obsessive emphasis on costs. Traditional HR management efforts end up being quite expensive, especially when carefully groomed individuals leave your company for the competition.

One of the essential elements of a talent management plan is talent acquisition. However, a lot of businesses don't invest enough time and energy in these procedures. Unfortunately, the continued fall in employee work satisfaction, employee turnover costing businesses billions of dollars, declining profitability, and the wave of Baby Boomer retirements have so far mainly eclipsed the good aspects of the "Talent Ecosystem". Many organisations lack well-thought-out and efficient talent acquisition plans. This might have an impact on both your business and you personally. It could provide your company with a significant competitive edge and boost your managerial performance.

Employee onboarding through the internet is becoming increasingly common. With the use of technology, businesses are smoothly onboarding workers from various places. In the post-pandemic period, talent management has taken on new dimensions such as virtual induction, training, and meetings. Make use of technology as a tool with the increased use of chatbots, the development of AI-powered solutions, and applicant management platforms and skills are transforming how businesses hire new employees. The problem, however, is making the most of HR digital investments to empower talent executives and the workforce.

You'll discover how to create a talent-focused recruiting strategy, decide which talent acquisition tactics are best in certain circumstances, and pick brilliant people who will fit in well with and significantly contribute to your business in this book. By using these tactics, you'll be better able to find the talent your company needs to support its goals by using these tactics. You'll also discover the value of talent management and its advantages in this book. As a leader, evaluate your department's or division's progress in creating a talent management strategy.

***Are you aware of the talent requirements of your business and are you assisting them within your sphere of influence?***

For talent management to succeed, it must be properly planned. It is vital and common to involve younger generations in talent-hunting. Our leadership is becoming older, and the skills gap is widening. There has never been a more pressing need to reduce the growing gap between human development approaches and business effects. The battle for talent is more complicated than ever in our contemporary corporate environment. For your business to succeed, you must be able to draw in and keep the best people, yet you cannot compete if you have the wrong strategy or attitude.

Historically, organisations have drawn a clear line between their talent management practises and their diversity and inclusion policies. The right people with the right talents in the right positions are needed by the company to enable operational success, which has been the driving force behind talent management initiatives. "Redefining Talent Management" provides a new viewpoint on why the current division between talent management and diversity and inclusion must vanish. You'll learn how to balance internal talent development with external talent acquisition in this book. Boost the precision of your talent-needs projections; maximise your talent investment returns; create an internal market that connects available talent to jobs to replicate the dynamics of the outside employment market. "Redefining Talent Management" provides you with the strategies and resources you'll need to match the talent supply to the demand for it today and in the future.

Almost always, a "talent" is the person whose contributions directly advance the organisation's or company's key goal, both current and in the future (or both). Therefore, talent pipeline might be defined as any proactive action that is necessary or directed towards enhancing the contributions or controlling the risks linked to important organisational functions and people deemed to have "talent." Simply put, "talent pipelining" is a proactive risk mitigation procedure focused on human capital and designed to guarantee the ongoing viability of the company.

Talent management needs to change from being hierarchical and bureaucratic to being flexible, strategic, and performance-based. It's time to change how you tackle this never-ending fight if your income is falling, you're losing market share to your rivals, or your organisational health is diminishing. After all, your greatest competitive advantage is people, not a product or service.

*"The recruiting process for that potential applicant will go more smoothly the more specialised your pipeline is and the more you tailor it to a particular function or competence. You must create candidate personas for talent pipelines in order for this to function. A talent pipeline works best when it is targeted. "*

*-Dr. Amit Das*

# Acknowledgements

At the outset, I will thank my family for supporting me throughout the journey of writing my book and encouraging me to live my dreams; my son has always been instrumental in giving his inspiration to complete the writing of this book. Despite the fact that I am listed as the author of this book, "Redefining Talent Management" would not have been published if I had depended entirely on my own talents. Creating this book required more than anything—it took a family of dedicated and caring people who were always prepared to lend a hand.

Writing a book while working full-time is no simple task, so I'd want to express my gratitude to my amazing coworkers who act as cheerleaders in equal measure. Thank you, too, to my students and clients for your patience and unflinching support while I worked on this book!

Thank you to everyone who has listened to me argue for doing everything you can to make your life, including your work life, more progressive. I appreciate everyone's assistance throughout the process. This book would not have been possible without each of you having had an impact on my life in some manner.

Lastly, I would like to thank all the people with whom I have been associated. You gave me power. I would like to thank Notion Press for publishing my book. Finally, thank you all for gifting your time to read this book.

I'd want to convey my heartfelt appreciation to the almighty God for bestowing his blessings and being so gracious.

# CHAPTER ONE

# Reintroducing Talent Management

*"It doesn't make sense to hire smart people and then tell them what to do; we hire smart people so they can tell us what to do."-Steve Jobs*

*Understanding the art and science of recruiting, nurturing, and retaining talent.*

In terms of talent management, this means that retention is crucial for every organisation and that doing so becomes a vital strategy. In my book, I make the case that you should tailor occupations to the contemporary workforce. You must pay close attention to each employee to see how the business can support their growth.

*"According to Wikipedia, talent management is the process of identifying a company's future human capital needs and making plans to meet them."*

Talent management and strategic workforce planning both include everything done to attract, keep, develop, reward, and motivate employees. The capacity of an organisation to find, keep, and develop the most talented workers on the market is known as talent management.

The global pandemic of 2020 taught us things that we would never have learned in business school, and we will never forget those teachings. Talent management, like other aspects of human resources, will need to be reevaluated and redefined in the post-pandemic future.It may not be a difficult climb to find fresh and good talent, but it is difficult to keep them on board. Talent management is a desirable ability to have. The fact that no one wants to lose bright and dependable employees is the root of the situation.

***As correctly said by Zig Ziglar, "People frequently claim that motivation doesn't last. Well, bathing doesn't either.That is why we suggest it every day."***

Talent management has grown in significance throughout time, and it will remain a crucial component of any HR strategy as long as we require a continuous and seamless flow of business. The term that follows provides a clear explanation of talent management:

> *"Talent management is the integrated collection of systems, initiatives, and cultural norms in a company in order to acquire, develop, deploy, and retain people to satisfy strategic objectives and future business demands. To keep us going, we all require frequent doses of motivation."*

The epidemic has changed the nature of labour. Talent acquisition professionals have modified their work processes such that they now onboard prospects online rather than in person. Workers will aspire to improved work-life balance as the workforce changes as a result of increased technological advancements. The majority of employees want to work remotely. A company must adapt and think about using remote or hybrid work methods while also reducing costs. With this money, technology might be improved to attract talent more effectively. Following COVID-19, a huge number of employees left their present employers in search of higher pay, more recognition, more flexible scheduling, and other perks. This phenomenon, known as the "great resignation," had an influence on numerous businesses throughout the world. The past two years have been the most challenging for India Inc., and they have taught us a lot about our identities as societies, as people, and as guardians of the weakest among us. It was a morality test to see what type of society we wanted to create after the epidemic. Transformation became a priority for many companies as a result of the irrevocable changes that the globe underwent. It is more difficult than ever for organisations to choose the best employees, support the digital transition, and enhance the employee experience. Empathy has made a comeback in the managerial vocabulary.

> *"According to the U.S. Bureau of Labor Statistics, a total of 4 million Americans will have left their employment by July 2021, a far greater rate of employee resignations than in the majority of economies."*

Organisations are compelled to turn to contingent talent given the agility and preparedness needed in a post-pandemic environment. Talent management strategy for the future organisations have the chance to remain ahead of the trends and competition for people as they battle a turbulent global economy, shifting work environments, and a competitive marketplace. They may improve business preparedness and future-proof their talent strategy by creating a more adaptable workforce, altering how they define work, and putting the necessary technology and data in place.

> *"Talent management that is effective and comprehensive benefits employees as well as the success of your company. In reality, businesses with strong employee management consistently outperform their rivals. However, effective talent management necessitates a rigorous and strategic approach."*

Today, most organisations worry about losing part of their talent through natural attrition. It is crucial to identify these gaps within the business so that you may either make an external recruit or take advantage of the chance to train and develop a high-potential employee. Offering a competent employee a chance for professional advancement is the best method to keep them on board, provided the necessary support systems are maintained to ensure their success. It's how your business finds and keeps the best employees. Finding top-performing individuals, supporting their success, and helping them find a position in your organisation to fulfil present and future demands are all made possible by talent management practises.

Employers are making more efforts to keep their workforce—or talent—at the forefront of many decisions. The focus is on identifying the best people and assisting them in developing, mentoring others, achieving personal career objectives, and assuming leadership roles. Retention is crucial for every organisation, and keeping people becomes a major strategy.

Organisations have been discussing the widening skills gap and the talent battle for decades. Despite the ebbs and flows of that discussion, little to nothing changed in the ways that businesses hired, onboarded, developed, and managed their employees. Even though times changed, businesses typically kept doing things the same way.

Now, business executives are also becoming aware of it. Leaders can focus on fostering culture wherever they are by not micromanaging, overcoming presentism politics, and learning to quantify what each person truly creates and contributes to the business with as much objectivity and facts as possible. Above all, leaders may improve the workplace culture even in a world where only virtual interactions take place by fostering justice and trust in interactions with employees. In post-pandemic talent management, the employee experience will receive more attention. Employers will need to develop strategies to improve superior employee experience across the board in the HR department as there will be fewer people available and the same amount of work to be done.

Redefined employee experience will become a bigger priority in talent management following the pandemic. Employers will need to develop strategies to improve superior employee experience across the board in the HR department as there will be fewer people available and the same amount of work to be done. It may not be a difficult climb to find fresh and good talent, but it is difficult to keep them on board. Talent management is a desirable ability to have. The fact that no one wants to lose bright and dependable employees is the root of the situation.

However, the majority of those individuals are either content with their current employment or actively seek out new chances. 2020 will live in our memories forever because of the lessons the global pandemic taught us—things we never learned in business school. Along with other things, talent management will also need to be reevaluated in the post-pandemic era. Examining how talent management will evolve in the post-pandemic period is important to pave the way for the interest of things, which has had a significant impact on the workforce's demographics.

Rapid change is taking place in the workplace. Massive changes in the workplace that were anticipated for the next ten years are now happening, and we must embrace them by making explicit investments in people management. My early experiences were very different from the present system, which has seen a continuous decline in the notion that the boss is always correct and a rise in the importance of the employee voice. Managers now actively contribute to bolstering and incorporating all voices, regardless of gender, age, or any other preferences. Employee-led initiatives are starting to pay off significantly in terms of retaining and developing talent.

Organisational talent management is under pressure from workplace changes, expected skills shortages, business impact, value generation, and shifting employee expectations. I've seen that talent in the new environment is more purpose-driven and intrigued by having a tough and meaningful job. And as leaders, that's where we need to continuously reevaluate and change our plan. Companies that successfully use skills in coaching for managers; agile talent strategies today spend money refining their managers' coaching abilities. I can't emphasise how much this is a welcome shift enough.

*"It is not surprising that businesses are investing more money than ever before in their employees management initiatives given how important employee engagement and productivity are to organisational success. As a result, talent management techniques have changed throughout time to reflect changes in the humanities. In the rapidly changing world of today, strategic talent management is required."*
*- Dr. Amit Das*

# CHAPTER TWO

# Redefining Employer Branding Strategies

*"Acquiring the right talent is the most important key to growth. Hiring was - and still is - the most important thing we do."- Marc Bennioff, Founder, Chairman and co-CEO of Salesforce*

## *Creating a positive employee experience is where a strong employer brand starts.*

In today's recruiting process, employer branding is extremely important and improves a company's capacity to draw in the best candidates. Cultural fit is more critical than ever for professionals looking for new opportunities as work and daily life become more linked.

*"Having a strong brand can help you recruit and keep the best people in the competitive labour market. Candidates want to work for companies that have a solid reputation—those that are recognised for their fairness, independence, flexibility, and strong leadership."*

In this chapter, I will talk about how to create an employer brand to draw in top talent and keep it engaging and current. I will also discuss what top talent takes into account when evaluating organisations as possible employers. Build your reputation as a top employer and become the organisation that people want to work for.

The reputation of your business speaks volumes about the values that your firm upholds. Whether a consumer uses your services again or writes a negative Your review depends on what is said about you online and how your services are viewed. It may also aid a prospective applicant in choosing between accepting a job offer and waiting for a better one. Because most businesses are aware of this effect, they work hard to attract clients via advertising, social media influence, and other marketing strategies. Your employer brand, however, is a frequently ignored area that calls for equal effort from your company. In this chapter, I'll look at the benefits of having a strong employer brand and the various ways in which this type of branding is important in the short and long term.

*"Your organisation's attraction to top early talent will increase if your employer value proposition makes it evident that your workplace is exciting and engaging."*

Your business will attract early top talent when you properly establish and create your employer brand, employer value proposition, and the messaging that goes along with it. This implies that job candidates will make an effort to differentiate themselves from the competition, making them difficult for you to reject. However, your business needs to be using its branding to do the same thing. Your organisation needs to put in a concerted effort to win over potential candidates.

I've authored several management books. I'll assist you in developing a new way of thinking about your brand in this chapter. I'm going to challenge the way you previously thought about your brand in this chapter. My passion is working with businesses to build your employer brands and reputations so you can draw in the finest talent they require. I'll look closely at what an employer brand is, why it matters, and the elements that go into creating one. I'll look at how some employer brands entice top employees, how it affects revenues, and why trying to imitate another company's brand won't succeed. I'll speak about an action plan to get you on track and produce results after I explain what creates a compelling brand and how to communicate it to the appropriate audience.

> *"A company's employer brand is how the people perceives what it's like to work there. In other words, it's the perception that potential, existing, and former workers have of their time working for your business. It depends on a variety of elements, such as your corporate culture, the workplace, and employee perks."*

I'll discuss how to effectively represent your business as a top employer and provide strategies you can use to enhance your standing in the industry. I'll also look at some well-known branding examples that your company might use as inspiration. Consider your employer brand as a rating system provided by present, former, and prospective workers. It encompasses all of the ways that your hiring procedure, office atmosphere, and even Fun elements influence employees' perceptions of the company. Maintaining an environment that promotes employee happiness has several benefits. Let me define employer brand and explain why you might want to start focusing more on this subject.

Each business has its own employment brand. Some have greater notoriety than others. Some of you might be thinking that since we don't have many vacant positions, we don't really need to spend much time concentrating on our employment brand.

> *"Strong employer brands, however, don't develop overnight. The fact that no one is leaving your company could change in the not-so distant future."*

When considering employment options, over 95% of workers in the workforce say that a company's reputation is a key consideration. Everyone from top talent to up-and-coming performers would thus likely avoid a company, regardless of how innovative their products are. Retention is one of the most crucial advantages of a powerful, good employer brand. As we previously discussed, the employer brand may determine whether a candidate chooses to accept a certain job offer over another. Creating and sustaining an employer brand that accurately represents your company's culture and values is essential for luring (and keeping) excellent employees.

> *"People will forget what you said, but they will always remember how you made them feel."*

Although a worker might not recall the precise terms of their employment letter, they will recall how simple it was to talk to a superior about a bothersome situation at work. They will always appreciate how simple it was to take a day off for mental health reasons and how paid time off is a common practise in the workplace. Very significantly, former and present employees will make sure to express their satisfaction with your company to potential new hires and anybody else who would listen. Employee recommendations are a reliable gauge of how well your company is performing in terms of employee relations and employer branding.

The advantages of having a strong employer brand are enormous: you'll waste less time and money on ineffective recruiting efforts, attract more top talent, and fill job openings faster since prospects will find you on their own. Since they are already interested in working with you, if top talent finds you rather than the other way around, you won't need to waste time searching for them. Your employer brand will develop if you use storytelling. Your company's communications must show that your employees are at the heart of all you do. You may accomplish this by: making films that include a welcoming face. sharing examples of successful employee cases. posting articles on social media highlighting employee accomplishments. The top businesses invest in their employees. Let's say you want to entice the top interns, students, and grads. In that case, you must produce content that emphasises the needs of your audience and demonstrates your commitment to them.

Ever wonder why certain businesses have top candidates vying for their available positions while others don't? You understand what I mean by those organisations where you would love to work. Those are businesses that have a solid employer brand. No matter how big or where they are—whether abroad or in your hometown—they have a reputation for being a terrific place to work. Companies with a good employer brand are known for looking out for their workers. There is a lot of work to be done, so let's begin. Imagine you just ran into a friend you haven't seen since college. That is what an employer brand is. If you're like the majority of people, your first thought is probably something along the lines of, "Wow, that must be a very wonderful place to work." Could you help me find a job there?

> *"According to the research, 75% of job seekers check a company's website and social media before submitting an application. Therefore, your online presence and how potential employees view your firm have a direct influence on the success of your organisation's recruitment efforts."*

It's critical to do a thorough evaluation of your website and social media to make sure that: This describes your strengths as an employer. This demonstrates your concern for your current staff's favourable narratives about your group and company. presents your perspective on work and business clearly. It conveys a value proposition for employers. Your digital platforms will be scrutinised by early-stage top talent to determine the nature of your firm. So that job searchers desire to join your organisation's "family," you should convey a strong sense of your corporate culture on these channels. Not only are your branding and messaging crucial to your business as a whole, but they are also an effective tool for hiring.

*"Many organisations find it worthwhile to speak with branding or marketing professionals in order to make sure that their branding strategy and communications are in line with their objectives. These professionals may assist in making your message compelling to the talent you're trying to attract and can offer significant long-term advantages."*

Establishing your company as a merit-based, equal-opportunity workplace encourages applications and contributions from people with all backgrounds. Incorporate diversity into all aspects of your business, not just hiring and recruitment. The experiences people have after they join your company will also be reflected in your employer brand. Diversity is a strong indicator of a good work environment, which is advantageous when trying to build your employer brand. The secret is to manage your employer brand so that you can be proud of how prospective, existing, and former workers view you—all of whom may turn out to be potential clients.

### Why is employer branding important?

The other day, I went to the grocery store to pick up a few items, including washing detergent. Of course, there were many different brands to pick from as I walked down the detergent aisle. I took the brand I rely on the most, and I set out to get the following item. I didn't even think about the possibilities for a minute. That is the strength of a powerful brand. A person is drawn to your goods or services right away because of the reputation you've built. However, branding is no longer limited to your favourite home goods. Branding is actually not just for companies anymore.

*"Good employer branding reduces spending on hiring and retaining employees. A poor reputation may cost you a lot, including lost sales and opportunities for growth. But most importantly, having a reputation as a business that doesn't put employee wellbeing first can literally cost your firm a lot of money."*

Employer branding is a certain strategy to put your business on the map in the eyes of employees. Your company will develop a reputation as a friendly employer if you appreciate the applicant experience, the onboarding procedures, and the best employee experience at work. Building an employer brand requires caution, even if it has several financial and human benefits. Intent is essential, but so are execution and consistency. This needs to be accomplished with the help of HR specialists and the finest recruiting marketing teams, and it should demonstrate a desire to encourage employee happiness and work satisfaction.

*"When you eliminate employee pleasure from your business identity, it initially keeps great talent away from your company. This therefore affects how much cash will be needed to recruit high-performing employees for your business."*

Employers with weak branding reportedly have to pay a 10% surcharge for each hire they make. When recruitment expenditures, testing fees, external agency fees, and other fees are taken into account, this may equal an average of $1000 - $3000 spent on each employee. With a good reputation, there is less bother and significantly reduced expense. When top applicants are certain that they will be treated properly and respected, they will immediately compete for positions in a company. Salesforce, first This company has won accolades for its ability to recruit both younger and older generations of employees.

So, you need to be ready to attract new people in a tight market. Start working on your brand today, and you'll be well positioned should you find yourself with unexpected job openings. Another reason to focus on your employer brand has to do with your company's reputation in the overall industry. Let's say a potential client is looking to purchase capital equipment from your company, and the equipment will require periodic maintenance. The client logs onto Glassdoor, an online site where current and former employees can anonymously post about what it's like to work for your company. The client also learns that your maintenance crew has a high rate of employee turnover. As a result, they decided to do business somewhere else. You quickly transition from being the market leader to becoming the market follower. Keep in mind that every business has an employer brand.

What companies prioritise and what millennials believe companies should prioritise are not the same. Employees nowadays desire fair treatment, the ability to significantly contribute to the organisation via their job, as well as adequate salary, recognition, and awards. They also want to feel respected and appreciated for their efforts. To ensure that employees feel a part of an inclusive culture, an organisation must provide a healthy work environment, put an emphasis on employee wellbeing, and create new opportunities. Finding experts, leaders, or potential executives for your business is the goal of talent acquisition, a continuous approach.

*"Organisations must develop a strong employer brand to recruit top people in a competitive labour market. Organisations must provide an explicit justification for why working there is worthwhile."*

Many employees prioritise their own needs, and it isn't necessarily a negative thing. I'll use one as an example. Kapil, one of my coaching clients, is responsible for supporting his aged mother and two college-bound children financially. Working with the blue chip company would make him happier than anything. Sadly, that is not his reality. His priority is his family. Kapil will be a dream worker for any organisation that is fortunate enough to secure him. When things get difficult, he won't give up, nor will he just relax and take it easy. This man is attentive. Since he has a lot on his plate, he must be. Let's assume for a moment that your company operates in an industry like financial consulting, where hiring self-centered job seekers is standard practise. You'll need to show that your company has exactly what a prospect like Kapil is seeking in order to get their attention.

Its employer branding places a strong emphasis on employee development, providing an opportunity for staff members to grow professionally and personally. Furthermore, Salesforce is notable for its interactive management system and charitable endeavours. Starbucks is an example of strong workplace branding. The company's employees are aware of the crucial role they play and are even given names in recognition of it. Employees at Starbucks express pride in their job. These feelings are expressed in business testimonials and on social media pages, where partners have their own accounts that are specifically for their professional and personal accomplishments.

### *What makes your employer brand so crucial?*

A few decades ago, it was completely acceptable for one employee to work for the same company while celebrating their 20th and 60th birthdays. Employee turnover has increased significantly over the past several years, nevertheless, as a result of job boards and other places offering current information on work possibilities throughout the world. The US saw 22% turnover in 2018, of which 15% were employees who left their jobs willingly. Companies reportedly lost $618 billion as a result of the latter shift. This is even more crucial in light of The Great Resignation, which occurred after the COVID-19 epidemic and saw a staggering 4.4 million US employees leave their positions, while the UK recorded one million job openings in the second half of 2021. Consider the numerous advantages of effective employer branding to fully grasp how branding is vital not just for your bottom line but also for the long-term viability of your organisation: It draws the most talented individuals.

Building a brand is crucial, but doing it well can benefit your company by ensuring smooth staff acquisition, engagement, and retention. Here are some pointers for creating an employer brand:

- You should concentrate on hiring people who share your organisation's goals if you want to retain current employees or encourage a collaborative environment. The same drawing board that has your company's values, purpose, and vision statements must be used again in order to do this. It is simpler to develop and build an employer brand that corresponds with these propositions if you can point to the core values and goals of your business to clients.

- Ask your team's rock star in the business to laud your praises if you have them. You need to emphasise how swiftly individuals are going up in your business if you want to attract the interest of employees trying to climb the corporate ladder.

- Include a chronology when showcasing the professional routes that a few of your top achievers have chosen. Remember that if you want to attract those egocentric applicants with distinct objectives from what has seemingly become the standard, you need to think a little bit differently. The good news is that all sorts of individuals will be attracted to your company by a competitive wage plan, quick career advancement, and the opportunity to work with superstars.

- Conduct a self-evaluation If there are no overt complaints raised regarding business operations, it is simple for employers to believe that employees are content with the current situation. Although assumptions are a good thing to have, they aren't always a true reflection of the situation, particularly when worker satisfaction is involved.

- Internal surveys, engaging reputation management companies, or even searching via social media searches may aid in assessing your employer brand to determine how it is seen by both existing workers and future job seekers.

- A first impression is something you can never get back. This is particularly true for new hires who may feel motivated to start looking for other jobs following a negative onboarding experience. Employers should see it as a good investment to go above and beyond to pique the interest of new workers in their positions. This entails making the appropriate introductions, giving them the appropriate tools, and educating them of all the benefits associated with assisting in the accomplishment of the organisation's purpose.

- When performing the same task for a while, monotony and drudgery are expected to build in. The onus is on the employer to continue to support ongoing employee development. This entails offering employees opportunities to advance their current talents and gain new ones. It also entails considering career options and ensuring that staff are informed about these professional growth paths. This can aid in avoiding complacency and boredom with routine tasks. Additionally, it helps keep employees motivated to advance their education and careers rather than merely hold onto their jobs at the organisation.

- Make inclusion and diversity a top priority within your organisation. A dedication to not only tolerating but also including, recognising, and valuing different individuals throughout the business is one of the greatest markers of a healthy employer brand.

An employer's value proposition can be thought of as a trade-off of the advantages an employee will receive in return for their services to the business. As was said, aligning business values with what an employer expects from employees is one of the first steps in developing an employer brand. When prospective employees are drawn in and keep an interest in the ideals and promises offered by the business should they accept the position, employer branding benefits. The advantages of your employer value proposition often match the goals of your business. It offers workers a compelling reason to continue to be enthusiastic and involved in their job for the organisation.

> *"A value proposition often aims to ignite employees' passion. It may not always be used to relate to monetary remuneration because it is linked to a feeling of meaning, purpose, and belonging."*

The human resource team or recruiters may share it with prospective and new employees because it typically works well with current workers. Consider being presented with a choice between two wonderful cups of coffee. One is fine, they say, and will put a little more pep in your step. The other, though, can increase the likelihood of experiencing stomach problems all day. No matter how wonderful either seems to be at the time, chances are you'd choose the invigorating coffee over the other one. This is how the bulk of the workforce evaluates job possibilities. Google receives millions of applications each year for a reason, and a big part of it has to do with their employer value proposition. This business has developed a reputation for being effective and inventive, which explains why people are so eager to be affiliated with it. Additionally, Google works to promote a healthy work atmosphere and prioritises the emotional health of its employees.

Employer branding enhances your online reputation. The last thing you want as an employer is for rumours to circulate about employee dissatisfaction and overall unhappiness at your business. The main goal of a corporation isn't necessarily to produce a fantastic product that provides value. It is essential to invest in and put a priority on the human resources that guarantee that not only are your products and offers up to par, but that you are also consistently innovating and providing fresh value that surpasses your consumers' expectations. Your brand could become unique as a result of this. The benefits of a good reputation are evident in the social media age, where organisations that put workers' welfare first receive quick praise, while brands that are found to be lacking in opportunities for growth and development, care and respect for employees, or those with subpar working conditions or unethical practises receive viral callouts.

Canva has preserved evidence of its kindness to employees. This business skillfully makes use of social media. Additionally, this company ensures that workers have a safe workplace and that their contributions are appreciated. Building a strong employer brand The moment to build a strong employer brand has never been better. Employees now have a stronger advantage in determining which businesses are worth putting their time and talents into thanks to groups like Glassdoor, LinkedIn, Hired, and more. Additionally, with the shift to remote work, office benefits won't be sufficient to make up for a work atmosphere lacking in respect, a sense of community, and possibilities for meaningful work and professional development.

> *"All reputable businesses must understand their brand identity and what it says about them. All reputable businesses should be conscious of their brand identity and what it says about the organisation as a whole."*

Today's job searchers have options. Companies are actively recruiting, and they are all vying for the same applicants. So, in order to get noticed, you need a strong brand. You can hire top talent more easily and affordably with the help of a strong employer brand. I'd like to ask you a question. Assume you are seeking work and receive two offers that are similar to each other. One is from Microsoft, while the other is from a brand-new business. What will you choose?

You are surely familiar with a business that is known for churning out employees. Would you jump at the chance if a recruiter called and asked you to think about working there? I'm assuming you would say "no" to the question. There are several employment vacancies available. Due to historically low unemployment rates, candidates have more options when it comes to picking their next employer because there aren't enough individuals to fill all the vacant positions. Therefore, if you want to acquire top talent, your reputation as an employer must be impeccable. One internal aspect that has a significant impact on how a company's employer brand is seen in the marketplace is its turnover rate. Review your hiring criteria carefully. Have you gotten to the point where you'll hire everyone that comes through the door? If so, stop. Warm body recruitment is never a good tactic and will simply increase turnover.

Even if they were already jobless, a staggering 69% of job searchers believe they would decline a job offer from a company with a bad reputation. This means that, given an option between two organisations, job prospects are likely to choose the one with a stronger market perception and reputation—in other words, the company with a stronger employee brand. Employer branding may provide a competitive advantage in the fiercely competitive job market by luring in top candidates as well as difficult-to-find, in-demand candidates and promoting long-term employee retention.

Where do you picture yourself working? What characteristics define an appealing employer brand? What organisation do you leave everything behind to work for, and why? The employer brand of that business is the manner. It has a strong employer brand if you drop everything to work there. And that is what your business needs. So let me share with you four fundamental principles that will aid in creating a strong employer brand. The applicant's experience comes first. I had a job interview with a reputable financial company early in my career.

You must assess and update your overall compensation packages on an annual basis. The market is only going to get more and more competitive, and the employees could feel a little let down by the recent lack of merit raises, bonuses, and/or salary reductions, which may encourage them to look for new employment options. Once more, it is the moment to make sure the compensation plan has a baseline to stay competitive. The involvement of the workforce in the company's strategy and growth goals is still crucial. Do they play a significant role and contribute to the greater picture? Are they subject to punishment? Do they occasionally face challenges? If not, the time is now to carry out all of these tasks.

In most situations, this will mean very competitive pay, chances to collaborate with top business leaders, and a quick ascent up the corporate ladder. Every one of these applicant requirements has to be reflected in your workplace branding. Beginning with your webpage One of your brand's main communicators is your website. It explains to applicants what they should anticipate when they enter your building. In order to effectively represent your company and the kinds of employees you want to hire, design your website accordingly. Candidates that prioritise their income and quality of life will want to know if this is part of your corporate culture. Make sure that the individuals in the photographs on your website are well-groomed, as opposed to a group of people wearing jeans and t-shirts. Show these folks eating lunch at classy establishments and driving good automobiles.

My suggestions for enhancing workplace branding:

- Make use of existing employees. When it comes to promoting your firm, billboards and sponsored advertising may be quite effective, but sometimes all that's needed are the stakeholders who have corporate ID cards.
- When it comes to sharing the outstanding work environment your firm fosters with others, employees represent an underutilised resource. Interested candidates can read testimonials provided by existing workers to gain first-hand knowledge of worker expectations. These endorsements could be shown on the business website's careers page.
- Employees may be urged to promote work activities and social outings on their individual social media pages. This enhances the genuineness of how employees view the workplace culture and may inspire a favourable perspective in visitors.
- Keep in mind that egotistical candidates care about material possessions. Also, if your compensation plan includes stock options and bonus eligibility, make sure to explain them. Sometimes all it takes to convince a candidate who is in high demand to join your organisation is the promise of working with a legend in their industry. An excellent way to draw these folks to

your business is to have videos and testimonials from some of your employees who are reasonably well-known in the sector.

- Give job descriptions more thought. Job descriptions are a good way to differentiate your company early on from competitors because they are one of the first points of contact throughout the hiring process. Job descriptions should be created by your human resources staff with the values and culture of the company in mind.

- To communicate to a prospect what could be required of the position, it can be necessary to use humorous or relevant language. Use social media-friendly techniques. When trying to develop a strong employer brand, social media and other forms of alternative communication are quick ways to influence how the job market sees your company.

- Having interactive sites on Facebook, Twitter, and even Youtube short or Instagram may do this. These pages ought to feature noteworthy workplace advancements as well as regular occurrences. You may use a corporate blog, newsletter, and other tools to promote the business as part of your employer's branding plan.

- Strong employer brand businesses continually monitor their surroundings, research their rivals, and make adjustments as they go. Reactivity is a trait of businesses that are less brand-focused. They won't make any adjustments until it seems like turnover is increasing or they see that a rival is hiring their employees.

- Companies that have strong employer brands are also excellent at marketing to their current workforce. They constantly serve as a reminder to employees that they've made the correct choice by showcasing not only the company's success but also their dedication to the local community, the health and well-being of their employees, and a bright future. Therefore, start by developing a strong employer brand if you want to draw in and keep talent, lower your hiring costs, and shorten the time it takes to fill positions.

- Numerous employers guarantee promotions following a certain amount of time spent working there. If it doesn't happen, the employees' trust in the firm is quickly lost. It doesn't take long until people realise that their promises are just hollow rhetoric. Because trust is based on keeping your word, the lesson to be learned from this is to be careful not to make commitments you might not be able to fulfil. Additionally, and significantly to job searchers, is how a firm is perceived in the neighbourhood.

- Employees are happy to brag about what a terrific environment they have to to work in. And both the employer brand and the firm witness exponential growth. Therefore, make an employer brand attractive by working hard to develop one. When you combine fun with work, you'll be well on your way to turning your business into a place where everyone wants to work.

- It's crucial to remember the ultimate goal when new solutions for talent acquisition hit the market, many of which are designed to address particular pain points: employing the tools in your HR toolbox to brand your business effectively. This will enable you to align with and filter items such that the platform disappears into the background while offering a top-notch candidate experience.

While recruiting focuses on filling openings, talent acquisition often concentrates on long-term planning and identifying suitable people for roles that call for a highly particular skill set. While recruiting focuses on the immediate, talent acquisition has a long-term perspective. Consequently, one of the key distinctions between finding talent and merely recruiting is emphasis. The hiring procedure itself is an internal aspect that affects corporate branding.

*Does your business, for instance, have a reputation for making recruiting decisions much too slowly?*

Your employer brand may suffer as a result. Take a look at the personnel engaged in making recruiting choices and get rid of those who are not necessary. Another internal element that affects corporate branding is employee absenteeism. I once worked in a department where there was a lot of absenteeism, which meant that we were all essentially working two jobs at once. Stress levels increased as a result, which increased absenteeism. No one in our department was willing to suggest our place of employment to others. This company made significant investments in its hiring strategies, but they overlooked a crucial aspect of employer branding. Maintaining your current workforce will enhance your company brand. We would have done our part to help draw in more new individuals if they had just made an effort to address the staff absenteeism issue.

The hiring procedure now heavily weighs the candidate's experience. Numerous reasons can lead to unhappiness with the hiring process, but two of them are frequently brought up on job boards: lengthy communication delays and the failure to provide rejected applicants with feedback. The practise of moving people up the corporate ladder without giving them proper training is one of the major blunders that many businesses do. When promoted to the next level, most businesses think that outstanding employees would quickly pick up the necessary skills. For instance, a top performer on the job might not make a great team leader and might only make a poor manager. Therefore, it's more important than ever to make sure the appropriate training and development programmes are established to maintain and develop the existing core people when aggressive expansion initiatives are devised.

Do you remember when you looked at a company and thought to yourself, "Wow, I'd really like to work there?" Those businesses are doing a great job of making sure they provide what employees want because they have a clear understanding of what they're looking for.

### How do job seekers assess potential employers?

Let me explain what prospects nowadays are truly looking for when assessing potential employers, so you may become one of those "wow, I want to work there" organisations. Companies must first fulfil a candidate's desire to get their fundamental requirements addressed. A candidate has to believe that a corporation can provide them with a remuneration package that they can genuinely survive on at this point. You've probably heard a million times that job seekers don't care about money. That is crazy. It matters, of course. Yes, today's job searchers do desire to work for businesses with a higher mission, but they must also be able to support their families, pay their rent, and make their student loan payments.

Employers don't have to spend time recruiting employees when their employer brands are strong. Job seekers look for them. Strong employer brands have access to a pool of talented applicants that are eager and ready. And each day, more people are lining up. A lesser-known firm must locate individuals and persuade them to submit an application. Moreover, it takes time. There are more eligible applicants who are ready and eager to work for companies with a good employer brand. A lesser-known firm must locate individuals and persuade them to submit an application. This requires time. Employer brands that are strong are proactive in retaining their employees. To stay competitive, they could design new programmes that provide employees with more chances to advance their careers, or they might introduce additional perks.

> "*A disgruntled and sceptical workforce is the result of companies that falsely portray themselves as employers of choice. And those employees are more than willing to combat the expensive branding efforts of their employers with more reliable word-of-mouth promotion. Let's imagine your business is one of many that has struggled in the past but is now prospering.*"

Candidates of merit do not approach companies that are in the headlines for unethical activities. People want their employers to act morally, treat people properly, and take initiative in their commercial dealings. And the people that make a difference in their communities are the ones who stand out for the right reasons. You don't have to be flawless or have the full package, but you do need to possess some of the qualities that today's job seekers are seeking when choosing an employer to work for. People will start to remark, "Wow, I'd really like to work there," if you step up your game. How to win over the egotistical candidates: While it's common knowledge that today's job hopefuls want to contribute to a better society, not everyone shares that desire.

The applicant's experience is what we refer to as It is the impression that applicants have of the company following the recruiting process. Companies that offer excellent candidate experience treat potential employees much like their consumers. Additionally, just as pleased clients will spread the word about your company, prospective employees will do the same. A strong employer brand is trustworthy. Avoid the urge to exaggerate and let others see you for who you truly are.

> *"Nothing can damage your image in the job market more quickly than putting a lot of effort into marketing a job experience that you can't actually provide."*

Your employer brand is greatly impacted by the employee experience. All those stock images of smiling people plastered on your career website won't be able to hide the unfavourable employer evaluations and social media buzz that disgruntled workers are publishing. Employer brands are stronger for businesses that focus as much on the employee experience as they do on the consumer experience. Asking your employees if they would suggest your organisation as a place to work will help you enhance the employee experience. Ask why not if someone hesitates or declines. Make a note of the input you get, then pick one or two items from the list that will have the biggest impact and advance them far more than if you picked ten items and advanced them very little. By continuously doing this, you'll raise employee happiness, boost retention, draw in better applicants, and see daily improvements to your employer brand.

> *"We will see increasing contact and engagement in the form of texts and SMS messaging in order to engage prospects we're seeking to recruit. By doing this, businesses will be able to re-engage candidates at any stage of the hiring procedure."*

So let's imagine your business is one of many that have struggled and is now emerging from the ashes. Whether you like it or not, a simple Google search will tell most people your story. Get in front of the situation and tell your tale the way you want to. Building empathy and trust may be greatly aided by a quick, two-minute video from the company's president in which you discuss your goals and aspirations for the organisation and its workers. It's something that many job seekers value and consider while choosing their future workplace. A strong brand tells a tale. Almost everyone is familiar with the tale of how Steve Jobs founded Apple in his garage.

> *"It's obvious that the focus is on making the work experience unique and authentic. Candidates desire a hiring process that works with their busy schedules and a genuine employer brand that represents the qualities they look for in an employer."*

What is the history of your business? What led you to become the person you are today? What difficulties did you have to get past? What does the future hold for you? And what kind of people are you looking for to help your company grow?

> *"A thorough grasp of the target market is one of the distinguishing characteristics of effective marketing. The significance of that strategy has permeated talent acquisition in a world where job searchers are also customers and have the same expectations. Businesses will tailor information like job vacancies and sponsored material to offer "world-class experiences."*

Employees are not only temporary solutions for getting talent; they are in it for the long haul. When a candidate is acquired rather than recruited, a number of factors need to be taken into account, including abilities, potential development, and cultural fit. Finding and persuading top personnel to contribute their unique abilities to your organisation should be the goal of your long-term HR strategy. When a candidate applies, he or she wants to know what to anticipate from your company, and your brand should make sure she gets that message.

Companies now have a wide range of alternatives to create mass outreach campaigns that are far too simplistic and work on a candidate-cultivating strategy. A typical organisation is structured to push brand benefits, but a candidate-cultivating firm is created to draw candidates (segments) by meeting their individual requirements. Communication is always reciprocal and as precisely targeted as feasible in a candidate-cultivating design.

The majority of the information that candidates need to be aware of comes from direct and indirect sources, such as corporate and career websites, specialised forums, social media, employer review sites, job boards, search engines, and peer-to-peer connections that control the cognitive elements of the brand image. You should have the ability to impact different touch-points once you've determined the candidate persona, the channels to choose, and the content buckets to concentrate on.

You must show that your business is a great place to work. The process of finding highly qualified applicants is quite similar to the process of finding new clients. Your acquisition plan must include brand marketing as a key approach. Spread the word about your tale so it becomes a legend within the company. The employment experience must also have been good.

*"One of the initial steps in attracting new talent is your employer branding, which is the marketing of your business. With the right branding, you can retain current potential employees, draw in more suitable talents, and make it simple for them to refer you to other potential employees. It may mean the difference between hiring the greatest talent and having it get away from you. By building a solid reputation, you may also more effectively set yourself apart from your competitors. The more talent you can attract and keep, the better your employer brand will be."- Dr. Amit Das*

# CHAPTER THREE

# Hiring A Multi-Generational Workforce

*"If each of us hires people who are smaller than we are, we shall become a company of dwarfs. But if each of us hires people who are bigger than we are, we shall become a company of giants."-David Ogilvy*

*Redefining recruitment strategies for multi-generational workforce.*

A workplace that employs people from up to five generations—Traditionalists, Baby Boomers, Generation X, Millennials, and the newest members of Generation Z—is said to be multi-generational. Companies can profit from the wide range of skills and life experiences that result in a workforce with various but complementary sets of aptitudes and abilities thanks to this type of work environment. Knowing the present talent pool requires, among other things, understanding the millennial and Gen Z job searchers of today. By 2025, it is predicted that millennials will make up 75% of the workforce, up from their present 35% share of the global labour force.

The COVID-19 epidemic, however, has caused a growing number of individuals to reconsider what they want from a job—and from life—creating a sizable pool of active and potential employees who are eschewing the orthodox path. What I am observing is a fundamental discrepancy between the number of individuals who are prepared to provide expertise and the demand for it from businesses.

> *"The epidemic forced individuals to labour indoors and remotely, which brought up a number of social and psychological issues. People end up working more and wondering what the point of their employment is as a result of the stress and fatigue that come with working remotely. The majority of houses are not suited for working from home. Families often don't spend this much time together. People, especially members of Generations Y and Z, require space."*

According to several studies, employees are eager to advance their careers. For many people, remaining with an organisation even requires it. Reskilling should not only be supplied on a selective basis in 2022, but also be deliberately ingrained in corporate culture and made readily available.

Hiring, borrowing, or sharing talent has already become commonplace in other nations. More and more businesses are collaborating with independent contractors so they can adapt quickly to new issues and bring in fresh perspectives. These "gigs" can target the staff members of the firm as well as other external parties. As a result, employees can take on responsibility for tasks in which their talents are especially applicable or test out new sectors for a while. Internal jobs encourage the creation of dynamic hierarchies and are a component of an active learning culture. As a result, accountability and decision-making authority are no longer rigidly bound to a role but instead vary based on the work at hand and the makeup of the team. Thus, work-on-demand is a key factor in helping firms become nimble and eliminate rigid silo systems.

> *"People are changing their occupations and sectors, transitioning into atypical professions, taking early retirements, or starting their own enterprises. They are either taking a break to take care of their personal affairs or going on sabbaticals. Hiring is more difficult because of the great attrition rate. Are the appropriate talent pools being searched?"*

In today's youth-centric culture, many organisations value the computer-and tech-oriented talents associated with younger generations of workers. There is little doubt that businesses in a variety of industries will benefit from the digitisation of the workplace in terms of competitive advantages. It would be naive to ignore the fact that older generations bring a wholly distinct set of abilities and a work ethic that also contribute to a positive and fruitful corporate culture. In the section below, you can take a quick look at some of the complementing abilities, attitudes, and skills that different generations of workers may bring to a business.

- Traditionalists (1925–1966): Despite the fact that the majority of members of this generation are retired or nearing retirement, having one of them on your team will impart to younger members of the workforce the realism, devotion, and tenacity that define these older employees. A traditionalist will undoubtedly also have a wealth of real-world knowledge that may be quite beneficial to a business.
- Baby Boomers (1946–1964): Workers from this age are highly motivated, competitive, and goal-oriented. Your team will be more committed to achieving certain professional objectives and aspirations if there are Baby Boomers on the team.
- Generation X (1964-1981): Gen Xers are often described as self-sufficient and practical. This group of employees will typically need less supervision and will be able to complete tasks quickly without requiring a lot of time or input from the management team.
- Generation Millennials (1981-1996): Anyone who born in between this perieod (ages 23 to 40 in 2021) is considered a Millennial, entered maturity at the dawn of the Internet era, will have cutting-edge technological abilities. This generation of employees is also incredibly adaptable and educated as a result of the significant changes in the workplace that they have witnessed and experienced. Although they inherited their parents‘ work ethic, they also tend to be accepting of diversity and inclusion in the workplace.
- Generation Z (born after 1995): The workforce of today is very technologically sophisticated. They are Internet-savvy millennials who can provide your business with

the competitive edge that comes with having a tech-friendly workplace and staff. Additionally, these staff members tend to be business-minded, so they will value chances to innovate within their line of work. In terms of the workplace, individuals of Generation Z tend to favour autonomy, flexible work hours, and ongoing management input. They desire employment with an organisation that is committed to their professional development and shares their values. The influx of this youthful and vibrant Gen Z workforce, which seemingly always has digital gadgets in hand, air pods in the ear, and a screen in front of them, has human resource specialists raised in traditional corporate cultures overwhelmed.

- Generation Alpha (2010-2025): The children that make up Generation Alpha are the first generation to be born entirely in the twenty-first century. They are surrounded by technology and are diverse in several important ways, including their race and ethnicity, family structure, and financial situation. Additionally, they are the first generation to have had their early childhood characterised by the coronavirus pandemic. There are 2.5 million births worldwide each week. When one age group transitions to another in 2025, Generation Alpha will have about 2 billion members worldwide. The beginning of Generation Alpha coincided with the release of the iPad by Apple, and the introduction of Instagram. This group has grown up in a technologically advanced environment and sees digital tools as more than simply a stylish accessory. Growing up online and connected, supported by tools like Alexa and Siri, and immersed in movies and all things visual, can have its benefits, including improved digital literacy and adaptability. However, experts caution that a childhood characterised by technology can also create challenges, including shorter attention spans and postponed social development.

So, it's time to reconsider our management philosophy and methods once more. With a median age of 28 years, India has one of the youngest economies in the world with a population that is over 65% youthful (between the ages of 18 and 30). This youthful population may be divided mostly into Gen Z and Millennials. In their efforts to keep work and home a little bit more distinct, Gen X and Boomers, who are currently in charge of many organisations, prefer the separation that the physical office offers.

### *What do various worker generations bring to the workplace?*

Combining workers from various generations; hiring workers from various generations and then placing them in distinct areas of your business would not make much sense. The ability of a multigenerational workforce to augment and complement one another's skill sets to boost output and produce excellent deliverables is one of its greatest benefits. Although there are encouraging instances of businesses that have successfully employed people from three or more generations, hiring and managing a multi-generational workforce can undoubtedly be challenging.

One company that often tries to engage workers of all ages for its warehouse management and logistics operations is Amazon Logistics. Both those who are just entering the workforce and those who are getting close to retirement and are searching for additional income through part-time work find the $15 an hour rate enticing. While employees from older generations provide stability and a strong work ethic that may influence other employees, workers from younger generations bring enthusiasm and tech-savvy abilities that keep the business operating efficiently. In order to increase productivity overall, initiatives like reverse mentoring and mutual mentorship pair up younger and older employees on the same shifts or projects.

> "*According to Younger, there won't be a consensus on how to "identify, explain, and assess the freelancing revolution" unless there is a consistent method. He writes in his conclusion, "What we do know is that, notwithstanding the controversy about how to count freelancers, it surely seems to be a vital and expanding.*"

Even though employee turnover is at an all-time high, businesses continue to use the same strategies to try to recruit and maintain employees. Employers still use the standard recruitment and retention strategies, such as pay, recognition, and career prospects. These aspects are crucial, especially for a sizable pool of employees whom I refer to as "traditionalists."

A new study identifies typical categories of workers that organisation may use to fill positions. It's the tendency toward quitting that just won't stop. As individuals continue to reconsider their personal and professional lives in the wake of the epidemic, the so-called Great Resignation may continue for a number of more years. In contrast to past downturns and upturns, this attrition is characterised by a large number of employees abandoning their jobs or leaving their employers without finding new employment. Some people who leave their jobs do come back, but only if they are guaranteed flexibility, sufficient money, and a manageable workload. Employees want to be treated with respect as entire individuals, not simply as cogs in the machine. They depend on their employers to create a strong workplace culture, a sense of camaraderie, compassionate coworkers, and career mobility, and they may leave if those demands aren't addressed.

### *Do you understand the mindset of new generations?*

Labels like "Generation Y," "Boomers," and "Digital Natives" are being phased out by businesses that are serious about diversity and inclusion. Instead, they accept individuals for who they are and where they are, and they foster environments in which workers of all ages, genders, and stages of life can contribute to the development of their careers. In this context, "human-centered leadership" also refers to developing innovative, easily available tools, learning environments, and work models, as well as encouraging an environment where staff members interact with each other with curiosity and openness. Both men and women must have equal access to leadership positions, and non-binary people should be a non-issue in 2022.

Starting your journey toward adopting employee benefits by surveying your present workforce to learn about their top priorities is a wonderful approach. According to LinkedIn, turnover was 56% lower for organisations with strong ratings for pay and perks. This statistic highlights how crucial it is to offer encouraging possibilities to keep workers motivated and eager to work. While Gen Z places the highest expectations on educational institutions (36% of respondents), Millennials feel businesses should be primarily responsible for training the workforce for Industry 4.0 (30% of respondents). The top three reasons for both generations leaving their present positions in the next two years are "unhappiness with income," "not enough opportunity to grow," and "lack of learning and development opportunities."

Job searchers are increasingly using social media, a platform that Gen Z and millennials are accustomed to using. According to Jobvite's 2019 Job Seeker Nation Survey, more than one-third of respondents locate employment prospects through social media, even though job boards continue to be the top option (69%). The majority of younger employees are also looking (41%). Increase your brand's visibility and appeal to contemporary prospects with talent management technologies that can link to these websites.

> *"Millennials are the backbone of the global workforce, transforming the labour demographics and being a priceless resource for every company. For an organisation to foster a culture where millennial employees believe their job matters, it need not be a non-profit or social enterprise."*

Millions of young people, most of whom belong to the Gen Z , will soon graduate from management colleges and enter the employees pool. Finding the ideal applicant for job openings at your firm is a far more difficult task now than it was last year. The epidemic has drastically altered the way we work and live, and as a result, we now refer to the present situation as "the new normal." An office may be on-site where employees work. Without a doubt, this new normal can provide difficulties for HR departments. The new workforce was very different from what people used to view as a typical workplace even before the epidemic.

A fresh approach is needed to keep Generation Z interested and engaged. Numerous studies have revealed that young workers consistently support flexibility and virtual employment. Tech businesses all over the world have announced workplace reforms to better suit the requirements of young people, which in turn supports their fast corporate growth. This is done in an effort to win the war of talent. In retrospect, one of the numerous advantages that are frequently offered to improve workers' work-life balance and boost staff retention is workplace flexibility.

***So, in this new business climate, how do businesses locate the ideal candidate for their openings?***

The answer is flexible, scalable recruiting technology. Restructuring the hiring process; most of the time, the hiring process is when the employee experience starts. The applicant has a chance to shine, but your organisation also has a chance to make a great first impression and highlight its distinctive qualities. However, using conventional hiring procedures won't get you there. After all, this is the new normal for us. Make sure your organisation stands out from the thousands of other businesses that are competing for the top prospects. Start with the social media platforms you use. Before applying for a job, Gen Z researches your firm on Twitter, Facebook, Instagram, and LinkedIn. Verify that they are up-to-date and align with your company's principles.

It's common for recruitment, human resources, hiring managers, training departments, and senior leadership to operate in functional silos. More integrated hiring procedures will increase HR agility and flexibility. The key to breaking through these barriers is shared objectives. Making decisions based on insightful data may be influenced by understanding what your company hopes to accomplish. With the use of HCM software that can deliver real-time statistics and dashboards, you can assess success and adjust to changing circumstances. Create solutions to solve problem areas, such as excessive staff turnover or delays in new employee training. It wouldn't be unfair to think of the freelancing revolution as having moved past the early adopter stage and now expanding. However, development does not equal maturity.

The impending Gen Z is another significant development that HR professionals need to be prepared for after the recent wave of changes to the recruiting environment. Relaunching career websites or enhancing the social media presence of your business are two examples. To learn how to successfully entice this new talent pool, continue reading. Technology has a similar role in the lives of the Gen Z generation to sleeping and eating. 96% of Gen Z members have a smartphone in their possession.

According to a Manpower Group study, workers' post-crisis concerns over flexibility are second only to their health. The majority of workers desire a hybrid workplace that combines work and home and promotes greater balance; they want to work remotely a few days each week. But there is still a place for personal interaction in the office. Ford and other businesses are using this as an opportunity to revamp how offices operate. Others are making investments in brand-new centres where people may interact and collaborate. The Gen Z workforce is most enthusiastic about returning to work (on their terms), and they, in particular, view the office as a place to socialise as well as network and learn.

Establish a systematic programme for internal hiring and encourage managers to alert staff to openings that could be a suitable fit. The fact that there is a 41% longer employee tenure for organisations with significant internal hiring shows that although managers are occasionally reluctant to urge their team members to quit their jobs, it is preferable to maintain the talent in the company than to have them search elsewhere.

Millennials and members of Generation Z are increasingly looking for meaningful work-life balance. They are driven to develop their talents, try out what they have learned, and take ownership of their professional development. Given this situation, fintech organisations that have a clear sense of purpose in the future will be able to draw in and keep the top personnel. This gives our IT personnel the chance to interact directly with the teams working on the product, business, insights, and marketing, which in our opinion fosters a strong feeling of ownership. They improve the workflow and get a deeper grasp of how products and services evolve. As your team members work closely together, they get an opportunity to go above and beyond the call of duty and get closer to realising your goal.

### *How can you deal or lead Gen-Zers better?*

More than 90% of the people we spoke with agreed that the company's employees were the reason they joined and stayed with their present employer. The folks they had the opportunity to talk with during their interview process and the initial months were the ones that had the biggest impact. Even when hiring a generation, employers should not undervalue the value of human relationships in fostering a great employment experience. Gen-Zers are highly motivated by a sense of purpose and a desire to positively influence their community and the environment.

They are more drawn to businesses that want to improve the lives of their customers, society, and the larger community.

Therefore, organisations must be explicit about their mission, objectives, and goals in their frequent discussions with staff. They will find significance in their work and experience greater job satisfaction when the younger workforce continues to establish congruence between their own ambitions and the larger organisational mission. Young talent is attracted to organisations that have a clear mission and set of values that demonstrate their dedication to their staff, clients, stakeholders, and the larger community, but what keeps them on board is how the organisation upholds its commitments in day-to-day actions, such as in town hall meetings and team interactions. A business must invest continuously to deliver on its promises, and the leadership and management teams are often held accountable.

This generation was raised with access to advanced technology and is knowledgeable and self-assured. The influx of this youthful and vibrant Gen Z workforce, which seemingly always has digital gadgets in hand, air pods in the ear, and a screen in front of them, has human resource specialists raised in traditional corporate cultures overwhelmed.

> *"So, it's time to reconsider our management philosophy and methods once more. These young guns' catchphrases include collaboration, active listening, adaptability, and digitisation."*

The majority of Gen Z were born between the middle of the 1990s and the middle of the 2000s. One distinctive quality of Gen Z is their high level of ease with technology and social media, as well as their familiarity with technology-driven globalisation. So, it can be said that Gen Z is the first generation to genuinely adopt a global culture in terms of communication and fashion.

> *"Tech businesses all over the world have announced workplace reforms to better suit the requirements of young people, which in turn supports their fast corporate growth. This is done in an effort to win the war of talent."*

Employers have found it difficult to draw in and keep younger workers since they frequently change jobs. Many of these young workers have seen a more glaring mismatch between what they want in a career and what their companies are offering since the epidemic, which has sped up the speed of their job switching. Data from LinkedIn indicates that the rate of job changes among Gen Z workers has more than quadrupled in 2019. Young workers are more receptive to new opportunities as the number of job openings has risen to or beyond the pre-covid level in several Asian countries, including Australia, Hong Kong, and Singapore.

> *"Employees from Generation Z are constantly looking for new challenges, so it's crucial to keep things interesting and novel for them. They are fearless and risk-takers. They view failure as a chance to improve and learn. In order to enable them to work freely and with greater responsibility, they want their supervisor to assign them interesting tasks with defined objectives."*

In contrast to being at the bottom of the ladder, Generation Z is more creative and would want to work on projects more autonomously and "own" them. They are prepared to give their all at work in exchange for potential rewards. Improve the way you distribute and manage your projects. Work on using Gen Z's ingenuity for the good of your business. The development of an idea from inception to completion fascinates Gen Z. Let them take part in the procedure.

Of course, managing Gen Z cannot be done in a one-size-fits-all manner like managing any other generation. There are many similarities among the younger generation that result from their shared experiences, despite the diversity of interests, backgrounds, identities, and other circumstances. Gen Z's collective experiences, which, like ours, have shaped common beliefs, routines, definitions of "normal," and general expectations, are reflected in a large portion of the quantitative data that is already available. One among them is their need for transparency and honesty. In order to gain and maintain Gen Z's trust, you must be H.O.T. with them, which stands for honest, optimistic, and transparent. You must be prepared to communicate honestly, support your claims with deeds, and carry through. Use "purposeful" leadership techniques.

Candidates at all employment levels are now more aware of these digital businesses thanks to the adjustments. Because of this, many proponents of workplace flexibility have argued that fully remote, hybrid work arrangements, and flexible work hours are the most important criteria for Gen Z to consider when evaluating an employer. However, are these the only things Gen Z wants when it comes to making a career move? While workplace flexibility is a major draw for many businesses, there are other critical considerations for young talent and new grads when deciding which organisation to join.

For instance, Gen Z and Millennials are likely burdened by student loan debt. According to one survey, the average American between the ages of 25 and 30 has debt that is about 69% related to education. While older generations of employees are interested in improved healthcare and decent retirement alternatives, Millennials, who likely have children, are more interested in life insurance coverage. Providing adaptable benefit options is a wonderful way to draw in workers from all generations. Give employees access to training and development. While our economy's digitisation undoubtedly creates new opportunities for businesses, it also necessitates the continuous development of new abilities and skills. Create training programmes for your current employees from all generations to keep multigenerational talent rather than "reinvesting" in ever-younger generations of workers who were taught the most recent skills required by our tech-oriented industry. Perhaps more importantly, companies that offer extensive and consistent training programmes earn more than 200 percent more per employee than those that do not.

> "*According to Lynda Gratton, a professor of management practise, the employment relationship between employers and employees is evolving. People used to toil in order to "purchase items that [made them] joyful. Today, however, the emphasis is on finding fulfilment in one's employment.*"

For more than 80% of both millennials and members of Generation Z, working as a gig worker is a viable alternative. Millennials actively change what is required for a positive organisational culture and advocate for balancing personal and corporate goals. They are also twice as likely to have a full-time working spouse or partner as Baby Boomers, making it harder for them to balance work and family in the previous five years. Additionally, many of them are caretakers for children and elderly parents.

For this generation, work-life balance or integration is crucial. Do not mistake their need for balance with "millennial sloth" or a bad work attitude. They don't seek strict separations between their lives and their jobs. They only want to be able to work more freely and evaluate themselves based on production rather than the amount of time they spend hooked into time-tracking software.

> *"Organisations must embrace "intrapreneurship" rather than discourage it, offer millennials the freedom to experiment, and give as much weight to a good idea coming from a highly experienced individual at the top."*

Rather than being confused about what they are doing and how it will affect the business, millennials will work harder, faster, and better if they see the value that they create. This generation is strongly motivated by profit-sharing, monetary prizes, stronger incentives tied to performance or goals, and friendly rivalry. The propensity of millennials to transfer careers, try various positions within an organisation, and change employment speaks volumes about their openness to experimentation and taking chances. They cannot survive in a society that penalises mistakes made when taking calculated risks.

Job responsibilities are not everything, as Millennial and Generation Z are demonstrating. They are more concerned with promoting the expansion and success of their business than they are with moving up the corporate ladder. They adore finding meaning and purpose in their work. The goal can be to improve the social or environmental situation, the business's bottom line, or the formation of a team. More teaching and direction in the form of good supervision should be given to them. Allow people to communicate their ideas and use their creativity in ways that benefit the company and their skill set. According to a recent poll, more than 75% of the workforce of the new generation would accept a job with several tasks in one location.

The availability of services that promote social, physical, mental, and emotional well-being has never been more important for millennials. Given that 20% of millennials are more likely than any other age to suffer sadness, according to a study, mental wellbeing needs special attention. Peer support groups, mindfulness exercises, and counselling are all very helpful in this endeavour.

Rewards and adoration should be included in expressions of appreciation. Praise for millennials' work in public venues helps them feel that their job has a bigger purpose, which improves their mood. Furthermore, what works for the majority of them is giving them time off to be their creative selves, to think outside of their daily chores, and to come up with something special.

Despite growing up with a lot of screen time, Generation Z still prefers in-person interactions. If your Gen-Z employee works remotely, video calls are preferred over phone calls. Plan frequent meetings with them if they work there, so you can get to know them and make sure they feel heard; these meetings might also be team or project meetings. They seek a personal connection and a sense of belonging.

This is not to suggest that you shouldn't employ a strengths-based approach; it just means that you must also direct them in their areas of development. Be ready to hear their opinions on what they would like from you as a manager or leader to help them advance as well. Ageism offends Generation Z quite easily. They believe that ideas and accomplishments should take precedence over age in the workplace. Despite their desire to learn and knowledge of their status as novices in the field, they want the opportunity to be heard and taken seriously. Invite your Gen Z employees to strategy meetings, pay attention to what they have to say about your business, and treat their opinions with the same respect as you would someone in a more senior role. Their depth of understanding and their logical yet audacious queries can infuse strategy with much-needed pragmatism.

> *"Millennials are frequentlyreferred to as the generation of quick gratification, whether this is accurate or not. They select recruiting practises such as responsiveness, quick feedback, and mobile- and technology-friendly job sites."*

What is regarded as "millennial entitlement" is a desire for development and advancement. According to studies, millennials are substantially more receptive to learning and entrepreneurship than previous generations. They frequently look for learning and professional development options that will enable them to advance in their jobs as well as experiment with and pursue horizontal ones. Give them difficult tasks, give internal talent mobility top attention, and make sure they have the necessary independence in their job. Giving them more control equates to releasing their powerhouse. They keep putting their best foot forward via ongoing learning and professional advancement. Every organisation ought to make an effort to adopt a disciplined strategy in this regard.

> *"Millennials currently make up the majority of the world's workforce and are fundamentally changing its composition. For an organisation to foster a culture where millennial employees believe their job matters, it need not be a non-profit or social enterprise."*

A few adjectives that best represent millennial talent are passion, spontaneity, boldness, digital savvy, agility, risk-taking, and catalysts of change. Millennials already make up the bulk of the global workforce, and by 2025, it's predicted that they will make up 75% of all workers. In order to create a workplace that is suitable for the future and to maintain a productive workforce, it is becoming increasingly important to successfully attract, develop, and retain millennial talent.

Flexible human resource policies and methods can help businesses recruit and keep a multigenerational, highly competent workforce that will boost output and enhance any organisation's culture. The workforce's flexibility is that employees of all ages value a flexible work environment. Employers may monitor the hours that their staff members put in while also allowing for more flexible schedules and various work habits by integrating digitalized employee time and attendance software. While younger, more tech-savvy employees may even be able to work remotely from their homes, employee attendance software can enable older generations of workers to seek time off in order to be more active in the lives of their children. A millennial considers more factors than simply the salary or the company's reputation when determining whether to accept an offer. A greater purpose than profit and success; how the employer brand aligns with their personal brand; flexible work hours; on-the-job collaboration tools; benefits that meet their social needs; value in the work they would be doing; demonstrating that you genuinely care about them; and the overall work environment are all important factors in attracting the right set of millennial talent.

Each generation of employees undoubtedly contributes unique abilities to the workplace, but they also have varied needs. Below, we provide a variety of concepts, plans, and policy options for enlisting, building, and retaining a multigenerational, highly productive workforce. People of all generations place a high priority on the benefits package. It's crucial to realise that various generations will value and demand different benefit packages.

Online tests that determine cognitive, behavioural, and skill levels are also very helpful during the employment process. To have a meaningful conversation with millennials, it's critical to help them visualise themselves in the appropriate position at the appropriate location. Technology has greatly empowered millennials, as it has all of us in general. They like maintaining connections online through both personal and business networks since they are social media savvy and cooperative. Therefore, it is excellent to engage on these platforms and develop interactive experiences with clear expectations given forth by the employer on the opportunity, the deliverables, and the what's-in-it-for-me. Online review sites like Glassdoor, LinkedIn, and Facebook Jobs are popular places to locate and recruit millennials. Employers may locate excellent full-time and freelance millennial talent on other well-known job sites, including Naukri, Shine, Indeed, Hirist.com, Angel List, Freshersworld, iimjobs.com, and freelancing markets like Upwork.

***How can businesses position themselves to speak the language of this burgeoning workforce and what do these generations value?***

Employee experiences as a whole and employee perks go hand in hand. More than ever, managers need to prioritise the emotional and physical well-being of their staff. According to 80% of respondents in a 2020 Deloitte poll, the success of their firm is significant or extremely important to their well-being. Working from home orders has a variety of repercussions on employees, as we have seen over the previous year. The balance between work and family life is becoming even more difficult for many to manage. Finding a solid work environment and taking care of family members at home may rapidly turn a scenario into a stressful one. No matter where your employees stand, it's critical to meet their requirements in order to maintain morale.

***In light of the significant talent shortage , how should business and HR executives update their talent strategies?***

Your company's capacity to recruit high-performing employees has an influence as well. It also requires a concentrated effort and a plan to handle these difficulties given the increasingly mobile workforce. The HR department of your business can better adapt to new problems and increase talent management key performance indicators (KPIs), including employee happiness, employee engagement, and attrition, by monitoring industry changes. The financial line of your business is impacted by employee retention, turnover, and hiring expenses.

Use a Total Talent Strategy to redefine work success will depend on how companies rethink how work is done when firms consolidate internal personnel responsibilities. Companies driving change are aware that there are various superior methods, and they use technology, data, and well-thought-out procedures to make these decisions. Through a developed whole talent strategy, leaders reimagine work, resulting in the trifecta of resourcing: finding superior employees more rapidly and affordably. More businesses are now willing to provide unemployed employees with flexible employment schedules.

Talent is encouraged by this freedom to think about alternative work hours, projects, job sharing, or even contractor status. Future workforce planning will heavily depend on knowing what talent is available and how quickly it can be deployed. Additionally, a lot of businesses are ingeniously reskilling and redeploying employees to areas where it is most required. In order to help people shifted to new positions succeed, they are also working to reskill them. Both permanent employees and temporary workers receive this treatment.

> *"To turn your vision into a reality, you must first take great care in selecting the ideal candidate for your business, and then you must involve them in training and development programmes in a methodical and scientific way so that they can consistently contribute favourably to the expansion of the organisation."*

According to the report, only roughly 28% of contingency employees were exposed before the epidemic. In the fourth quarter of 2020, the percentage rose to 44% following the epidemic. Permanent flexible work arrangements are only one part of the process of reinventing work, though.

Employee reward programmes for eLearning are just another fantastic approach to keep everyone happy. Employees can earn points redeemable for rewards by doing well on examinations and other training programmes. By employing leader boards to monitor employee growth, it also fosters constructive rivalry among colleagues.

Many businesses prioritise the well-being of their employees through programmes including providing mental health coverage, setting up areas for constructive peer interaction, and providing flexible benefit plans that are tailored to their individual requirements. 70% of a survey results believe they lack most or all of the skills needed for Industry 4.0, the most recent stage of the Industrial Revolution focused on technological advancements and the utilisation of cyber systems. At least 800,000 more candidates visited Airbnb's recruitment page after they revealed earlier this year that its workers could choose where they wanted to work and live anywhere in the world.

Despite the limitless opportunities that digitisation offers, far too many individuals are still working constantly at their maximum capacity and scarcely have time for all of the interests and desires that are still unmet in them. The 40-hour workweek has run its course. With less but wiser, more cooperative labour, many objectives may be accomplished. However, only if the ongoing interaction with several teams does not become a chore in and of itself. Companies must teach staff to utilise digital technologies and to communicate with one another, for instance, when it comes to providing positive feedback or declining requests from coworkers. We shall be much closer to the original vision of "New Employment," where paid work takes a backseat to what individuals "truly genuinely" desire, thanks to the ensuing freedom.

> *"Evaluation of an organisation's hiring, interviewing, performance management, and promotion procedures is a key component of a complete plan for spotting biases and flaws."*

Discuss how your business promotes the physical and emotional wellness of its workers through internal initiatives that promote wellness. As a demonstration of your company's ideals, invite the candidate to check out your company's social media channels. An ideal worker from the 1950s would undoubtedly be astounded by the current state of work as if they were in a Black Mirror episode, with its dependable video conferencing platforms, digital collaboration software, widespread cloud-based connectivity, and data-centric approach to strategic decision-making. However, it required a pandemic to really accelerate this tendency and revolutionise how most people go about their daily work, using these fundamental characteristics of technology to profoundly and maybe permanently alter how we approach our professions and lives. Indeed, the recession has accelerated a long-desired transition toward more flexible employment and the ability to live one life that better combines work and home for individuals who have the necessary ability to work remotely.

Employees may take advantage of training opportunities and prevent burnout with the aid of promotions and transfers. Faster talent management procedures Getting individuals into the correct positions and swiftly deploying them is the first step in making the talent management procedure more agile. You need to communicate clearly and succinctly to achieve this properly. Instead of relying just on quarterly or annual assessments, take into account an iterative approach to assessing talent requirements and continuously gather and evaluate input from and about employees. Pay special attention to non-traditional career paths because there aren't enough truck drivers in the United States. Millions of potential drivers—women—attracted to the promise of consistent schedules and competitive pay were being overlooked by logistics and transportation companies in a traditionally male-dominated industry.

> *"Fundamentally, culture may be defined as "how we do things around here." Whether or not people visit an office often, each business has its own distinct environment due to its default habits, preferences, beliefs, and decisions."*

Organisations have a rare opportunity thanks to this "talent uprising" on a number of fronts. At the beginning of the epidemic, many quickly shifted to a remote work setting, demonstrating that employees do not always need to be "in the office" to succeed at their employment. This has made it possible for businesses to hire the finest employees from places other than their usual neighborhoods, and not only those who live locally or are prepared to migrate. This has given rise to a fast-paced potential to make significant changes in corporate culture.

> *"The organisational culture, which is essential to supporting the successful implementation of a business plan, must also continue to change as the business strategy does."*

This is a chance for leaders to refocus their organisation on a desirable culture that is driven by leaders, supported at every stage of the employee lifecycle, and made possible by excellent HR. You may be familiar with internships; however, the newest trend of "returnships" is a little different. The most recent additions to the labour market are people who have taken a lot of time off or who have recently retired, not students or fresh grads. A multigenerational workforce, according to nearly 9 out of 10 talent professionals, makes a firm more successful, so think twice before you start thinking of it as volunteer labour. A smart and deliberate approach to employing a workforce with a variety of experiences is a potent tool for building teams.

> *"Gen Z wants to see real-world examples of how their skills may be applied. Given their strong desire to succeed, it would be useful to define success precisely and then demonstrate how to achieve it."*

Next, capitalise on their advantages by assigning them to jobs or tasks that will best display their talents. In addition to your suggestions, Gen Z will be looking for honesty, openness, and transparency. Due to Gen Z's need for critical feedback, a traditional strengths-based approach does not resonate as well with them. Make sure they are engaged, above everything. Consider posting videos of both seasoned workers and recent hires discussing why they enjoy working for your business, as an example. Keep in mind that your company's image will be reflected throughout the whole hiring process.

> *"Technology and the global health problem have greatly reduced the amount of corruption, nepotism, and poisonous politics, which is a fantastic silver lining."*

According to a LinkedIn report, businesses with superior training had an attrition rate that was 53% lower, which lowers hiring expenses and boosts productivity. Training and reskilling are crucial since both employees and organisations need to remain up to date on the latest technologies. The importance of diversity, equality, and inclusion (DEI) extends beyond effective public relations. Your business may offer a more comprehensive view and approach to everything from customer service to marketing and problem-solving by concentrating on the characteristics and backgrounds that make individuals distinctive, such as race, age, religion, disability, and ethnicity. You may use that variety as a resource to further your company goals.

Many of the same technological advancements that are changing the nature of the workplace may also be utilised for creative training. For instance, compared to a conventional film or book, augmented reality may provide employees with a better, more realistic experience.

DEI is a tactical and financial benefit for firms, and it's quickly gaining importance among candidates for jobs. For instance, a rating for employees' satisfaction with DEI is currently available on Glassdoor. In addition, research by HR consulting firm Deloitte found that nearly three-fourths of businesses that pride themselves on having world-class people management programmes prioritise gender diversity and international diversity.

Diverse viewpoints and life experiences might be beneficial to your company. A diverse workforce makes for deeper discussions, better-informed decisions, and a stronger organisation overall. In fact, diversified businesses had a 33% higher chance of outperforming their rivals. Start by improving your communication. Get a sense of how your business is doing, put DEI metrics in place for hiring and retaining staff, and work to diversify your applicant pool. Send surveys to employees, form employee resource groups, and host town halls to discuss the issue. A slew of events over the past couple of years have thrust the diversity debate front and centre.

*"Concerns about DIBs (diversity, inclusion, and belonging) are top of mind. 77% of talent professionals, according to LinkedIn, believe that diversity will be crucial to the future of hiring."*

When everyone is seeing you on a Zoom call, it is more difficult to play office politics, brag, or manage up. Additionally, the ability to record, record, and analyse meeting data gives businesses the factual data they need to assess DE&I in real-time. Diversity analytics, which includes a measurement of how frequently members of various groups speak during meetings, whether they are included in or excluded from the informal social networks that control an organisation's power dynamics, and whether the group values their ideas and comments, has the potential to speed up progress in a still dysfunctional area. The fact that technology and the global health crisis have largely sanitised the toxic politics and nepotism that undermine the meritocratic ideal of talent-centric organisations is a wonderful silver lining because it makes it much harder to "pretend to work" when no one can see you or cares where you are.

In 2021, demand for cloud computing expertise peaked. While this is fantastic news for people who have the necessary technological abilities, it is less promising for businesses. Talented individuals won't wait around for you in a competitive market because of this. Business executives are increasingly thinking about DEIB, or diversity, equity, inclusion, and belonging. However, organisations must evaluate, analyse, and report on these characteristics with far greater sophistication and efficacy than ever before if they are to affect significant change.

In order to gain insights into where inclusion is lacking and thriving as well as the various experiences of inclusion across employee groups, organisations are now looking beyond representation and capturing key indicators such as retention rate, employee engagement, internal mobility rate, inclusion scores based on diversity perceptions, and equity in pay. This market's expansion demonstrates the demand for tools that may help businesses address D&I concerns. Utilizing D&I technology has benefited companies like Accenture and Johnson & Johnson. Adopting such solutions will be crucial for businesses to promote a more diverse workforce. For a very long time, organisations have used representation to track and evaluate their progress on diversity. Representation is important because it gives historically underrepresented groups a voice. An organisation's competitive edge in a more globalised environment is the variety of techniques and various viewpoints that are accessible from the backgrounds and experiences of the employees.

The majority of organisations believe that only race, gender, and ethnicity are considered to be part of diversity and inclusion. However, the idea of universal equality among its employees is what separates a strong corporate culture from a terrible one. This includes age, which is sometimes overlooked in D&I activities; gender; sexual orientation; religion; and physical limitations. Recruiting discrimination against senior employees is most common simply because of their "age." Organisations must focus on the experiences that age offers rather than just age as a number. Longer lifespans and the current state of the economy are factors that are fostering the expansion of this skill pool. Nevertheless, while bringing talents to the table that can only be developed through years of exposure to problems specific to their business, this seasoned workforce nevertheless constitutes an underused group. Ignoring the potential of experienced individuals in a market that is becoming more competitive and fast-paced might really be detrimental to a company.

Talent recruitment requires a lot of effort and resources. According to a recent industry study, recruiters typically spend up to 13 hours a week hiring for a single position. Organisations must take advantage of technology to streamline processes, eliminate menial tasks, and give recruiters more time to interact with applicants. Technology may also speed up and improve procedures so that qualified applicants are never passed over. An application tracking system (ATS) is software that aids in monitoring your whole hiring procedure. As a consequence, it helps manage prospects, shorten the time it takes to fill positions, and speed up the hiring process. A more technologically oriented approach to hiring is now possible thanks to recruiting tools, digital platforms, and automation.

Employee recommendations can include a wealth of amazing talent leads. Many big and small businesses regarded employee recommendations as a vital source of excellent talent. Encourage your staff to recommend job prospects they think would be ideal for the position. If you want to get more responses to your request for employee recommendations, you may consider rewarding workers who recommend applicants who end up getting hired. Consider fostering applicants that performed well during your hiring process but were unsuccessful by interacting with these individuals and maintaining the dialogue so your business stays top-of-mind when next openings become available.

Another significant area of automated work is hyper-automation. So bots are being given transactional jobs, so they may improve employee experience by giving staff members the information they require right away. Before conducting in-person interviews, chatbots can engage with qualified candidates to shorten the time-consuming recruiting process.

Internal recruiting speeds up onboarding and improves employee engagement. As they remain with the firm longer, it gives the employees opportunities and helps to lower employee turnover. The best and most objective talent identification outcomes come from using evidence-based data rather than intuition. Assessments are founded on science and technology, are data-driven, and provide a superior experience while still retaining a human element to the process. This aids in increasing process transparency. More significantly, the data must be accessible in real-time to provide executives and HR the knowledge they need to make decisions. More significantly, real-time data access is required to give HR and leaders the information they need to make people-related recruiting, re-deployment, and succession decisions. The third year of the epidemic will be 2022.

In the new normal, recruiting managers will have the authority to use objective facts rather than just opinion when making talent decisions. Processes for managing talent would now lead to more responsibility on both sides of the process. Because companies succeed when people succeed, the HR departments of the future will use the lessons learned from consumer marketing in their operations to develop effective brand ambassadors from their workforce and have a greater impact on the organisations.

To locate potential applicants, HR searches LinkedIn and social media. These platforms, however, are no longer able to meet targeted criteria because they are too big, crowded, and irrelevant. Sector-specific platforms are popular for meeting business needs. These platforms are fostering strong employer-employee relationships and encouraging meaningful interactions, which may assist executives in finding and attracting employees who will fit into teams and improve the working environment. Technology and human resource management are interwoven in many ways. The industry, and particularly talent management, is going through a significant transition. Organisations that implement these changes and continue to innovate their human resource management strategies will be better positioned for long-term success. And that process begins with selecting the appropriate technology and solutions that can enhance employee experience, promote staff engagement, improve diversity in the workplace, retain and recruit personnel, boost productivity, and do so much more.

Finally, during the hiring process, show that you care about the candidate. Respectfully respond as soon as you can to any emails or texts sent to you by prospective employees. Comment on the opportunity and the interview. Maybe this applicant isn't the best fit for the position. However, he or she could know someone who is or has applied for a different position with your business. An unfavourable hiring procedure may be the deciding factor for a job applicant. Developing a culture that will keep your best employees. You should confirm that your new Gen Z recruit intends to stay once they have been onboarded. According to several studies, individuals in this cohort want to change jobs within a year or two after starting work if the position doesn't allow for promotion or doesn't help them build their leadership abilities. They're more than eager to switch between jobs until they locate the ideal one. The appropriate talent will be drawn to the right culture. Companies, however, frequently presume that culture is uniform. Culture is resistant to change, much like the people that make up a unit. The task of ushering in a new era of a sustainable, organic, and healthy work culture falls to the leaders of this frontier, the managers of human resources.

*"The challenges businesses face with the skills deficit are intensifying due to the continuous exodus of baby boomers from the workforce as well as required stay-at-home orders that force people to assume several responsibilities. These two factors have caused the skills gap to widen."- Dr. Amit Das*

# CHAPTER FOUR

# Nurturing and Empowering Talent

*"Train people well enough so they can leave, treat them well enough so they don't want to."*
*-Richard Branson*

*HR can play a crucial role in enabling and retaining talent in an organisation.*

Talent management has been changed by the pandemic. A continuum with two extremes describes it. One is what we refer to as the exclusive approach to talent management, in which you concentrate on a limited number of high-potential workers, most capable employees, and employees who are more valuable in terms of their performance—what they offer to the businesses. The inclusive approach, on the other hand, makes the case that everyone is gifted and should be handled according to their skill set.

*"Human resource management is then known as HR, and some individuals contend that talent management is a new name for HR."*

In accordance with my theory and the way I teach it, talent management is a branch of human resource management that concentrates on your most important workers. The argument is founded on the exclusive approach, which holds that talent should be handled in accordance with his or her value to the company and that a limited number of really talented individuals in crucial or important roles make distinct contributions to organisational success. similar to Pareto's Principle or the 20/80 rule, which states that 80% of a company's revenue or profit comes from 20% of its employees.

HR is crucial in developing leaders with the right qualities and in keeping the best employees in the company. HR solutions can support HR leaders in creating and managing teams, getting the greatest performance out of them, and contributing to the overall productivity and expansion of the business. The talent management landscape of today is defined by the fact that "change is the only constant" due to shifting worldwide work patterns. Flexibility, work-life balance, and a positive work atmosphere are equally important to young professionals as an alluring compensation package and career chances.

> *"Talent management is a dynamic process that will continue to be a somewhat difficult path ahead in the futre, but it will undoubtedly be an exciting one as well."*

Let me state the obvious first. The Indian economy and jobs remain difficult as the calendar turns. To combat this climate, it is crucial for leaders to continually engage staff members and communicate the proper message about the organisation's primary objectives and initiatives. Without suggesting any significant changes to the organisation's basic principles and employee-centric policies, this can entail tighter KRAs and process simplification.

Due to the shifting demographics of the global workforce, workplace diversity and inclusion are more of a requirement than a choice. In reality, the shift in demography reveals that a greater share of educated and talented workers, who will also be tomorrow's customers, are coming from developing countries and communities. Therefore, it is crucial that communities develop workplace integration skills and enable everyone to steadily ascend the social and economic pyramid. If your business wants to promote more diversity, you might wish to think about your system's present capabilities and whether or not diversity initiatives are supported by them. Building a broad talent pipeline is crucial since it's sometimes against the law to display preference in hiring. A new technology sector has emerged in response to diversity and inclusion (D&I) challenges to assist enterprises in overcoming weaknesses.

> *"Flexibility, work-life balance, and a positive work atmosphere are equally important to young professionals as an alluring compensation package and career chances. Remote work and team projects are rapidly taking the place of the conventional "office," and smart technology is driving facilities management."*

The epidemic and how HR directors are reacting to the ensuing new work paradigms have contributed to the newest developments in talent management. I've put together this brief look at the key emerging trends in talent management to help you understand what this exactly means, how to compete for increasingly hard-to-find talent, keep the talent you already have, and make sure your people are engaged and have a clear career path in your organisation.

The HR staff places just as much importance on an employee's financial stability and professional development as they do on their mental and emotional well-being. An open-door policy, which many firms have implemented, will encourage new-age workers to share their thoughts, views, and ideas. Globalisation has become the new standard, and businesses are now engaging with customers both inside and internationally, which requires a solid digital foundation to increase efficiency. If e-commerce was the rage five years ago, artificial intelligence is now (AI).

Leaders must understand that while some employees may still desire to visit the office sometimes, relatively few do so on a daily basis. Flexibility in scheduling will be crucial for occupations that need physical presence; flexible shifts will allow parents to work part-time as instructors; and flexible days will allow the workforce to work in a way that supports life.

To increase workforce flexibility to improve workforce sustainability many businesses included contingent employment in their strategic planning, and many of them even had plans to investigate it before the pandemic became a significant concern. "Workforce" is used to refer to full-time, permanent employees. However, many companies no longer operate in this manner. The epidemic has motivated organisations to speed up their transition, and some will likely shift their employment model permanently.

According to a survey report, businesses are eager to employ both flexible and long-term employees. About 51% of managers have combined internal duties for temporary and permanent employees. As a result, a lot of businesses have also been pushed to think about how to employ talent, curate it, and redeploy it wherever it is required as a result of the increased interest in direct sourcing of contingent labour. The existing approach does not enable an optimal talent strategy; therefore, firms will also need to consider how they will redefine work to capitalise on the accessibility and flexibility of contingent personnel. Leaders and recruiting managers will need to dismantle silos and consider how various work arrangements might provide greater results than standard hires in order to maximise contingent talent.

The beautiful thing about video calls is that the boxes are all the same size—it's a terrific equaliser. You had all your employees participated in meetings before the crisis, when some of the team were there in person and some were online. The online participants mainly watched the conference from a distance. Being "in the room" was a benefit, much like being in the right location at the right time and speaking to the right person. But you should be adaptable enough to let the workforce function in a way that promotes life.

HR's position uring the Covid-19 era, it became very evident what HR meant today. There are now more than just administrators and recruiters working in this field. They are crisis managers, consultants, and specialists in digitization and education. They act as the company's heart and soul, giving workers a voice in the business. In the future, judging the quality of the work experience and capturing the voices and emotions of the organisation will be even more data-based and less intuitive. To achieve this, HR is creating procedures and technologies to collect input and comprehend what workers require to feel good, be successful, and be eager to collaborate.

> *"As a function, HR must keep this in mind because, in addition to managing the company's most valuable resource, they also work to enhance the company's reputation. Additionally, they must "handle with care"!"*

More precisely, firms may now use AI-powered solutions to simplify hiring, onboarding, learning & development, and performance management. This is just one example of how AI can completely revolutionise an organisation. AI can also help automate repetitive operations, identify individuals who are likely to leave their jobs, and we could soon see virtual assistants powered by AI aiding communication and training programmes.

Numerous businesses have stated that they either already have or will have a skills gap in the next few years as a result of the rapid rate of change we have seen in recent years. The organisation with a comprehensive perspective of their workers' current skill sets and an understanding of the talents their people are interested in acquiring as part of their future steps are most prepared to cope with the realities of shifting skill landscapes.

### How can HR make a big difference?

A human-centered approach to corporate resource management and human capital management that allows you to track personnel and resource availability data for your employees as well as skill data. Giving executive teams and stakeholders access to a single source of truth for talent management, that transforms information that is typically seen as belonging to the "soft side" of HR into dependable numbers and metrics that are easily utilised to support a business case.

In 2022, HR work will not be complete without implementing people analytics for the "People", which is the ethical collection of employee data, its analysis, and translation into actions that concentrate on the people in the firm. Additionally, department managers must be enhanced in their capacity as mentors and coaches since they serve as crucial points of direct communication between the "HR control centre" and the workers.

HR is requested to offer assistance and find qualified individuals to fill managerial roles in this situation as well. By doing this, they may find and develop talent on a decentralised basis, and HR will have less "control from above" and more time to focus on strategic workforce planning challenges. When considered collectively, all of these actions ultimately determine whether a business can recruit and keep talent, thus assuring its success. Internal structures need to reflect this demanding function of HR. A new perception of human resources (HR) as a professional service organisation with consultants, product managers, service personnel, and tech specialists who should always be present at the table as partners with the management in crucial decisions.

Traditional hiring practises frequently place a strong emphasis on a candidate's education and experience, but these factors don't necessarily indicate what skills an employee possesses. Companies must understand what talents are in great demand, who possesses them in their workforce, and where training or new recruits are required in the present talent-scarce economy. Traditional worker management solutions don't have the data. In order to close the gap, the HR tech sector developed a new tech category. Talent marketplaces and skills management systems both promise to alter the HR tech marketplace.

> *"To provide your team with timely feedback and assist each member in understanding how their work fits into the larger context of the business, you must have a performance management procedure. The remote working environment added a significant complication to the procedure."*

In this digital economy, learning new skills is a fiercely competitive endeavour. Training and upskilling are more crucial than ever for staying employable as a result of unexpected technological innovation. We must simultaneously try to make the workplace, as well as the environment around us, more diverse, inclusive, and kind. Therefore, in order for businesses to advance into the next decade, staff members must use cutting-edge technology and adjust to the rapidly changing environment in order to reduce absenteeism and boost productivity.

Employers must support employees in achieving this by promoting physical and mental health as well as work-life balance. Social media has been a crucial tool over the past few years, offering people & culture teams a window into the potential employee's thoughts. Data analytics may be employed in 2020 to comprehend reward and performance programmes, staff attrition, and retention. Along with recruiting and retention, predictive analytics may be used to improve systems for talent review and objective evaluation.

The nature of your work is currently being renegotiated by you all. You're having in-depth discussions on where the job needs to get done. And this is all happening as businesses cope with the realities of teams that are more globally linked and operationally burdensome due to the significant increases in compliance requirements.

> *"HR leaders have access to a wide range of HR technologies, including workforce analytics, predictive analytics, NLP, and AI-driven prescriptive analytics."*

HR professionals should thoroughly comprehend and use these technologies for the sake of the people and company. How well it satisfies the unique requirements of each business and its constituents is at the heart of a successful transformation of HR technology. Technological advancement creates solutions that are tailored to each organisation's unique requirements in order to properly account for the context, culture, and procedures while building the solutions.

> *"Technology may be a crucial facilitator for designing the ideal employment experience. It may have an immediate effect on productivity metrics, support staff development, and aid in attempts to design career paths. HR teams must actively use the data and insight from these technologies to improve talent strategies for engagement and retention."*

Today, the majority of knowledge work is already project-based. Then, you need to take a precise inventory of the abilities you now have inside your company, including not just those that are mentioned in your job descriptions but also any hidden talents your employees may possess, even if they don't appear to be currently applicable.

### *How do HR departments actually do this?*

First, you need to turn as much of your work as you can into projects. Take a full-time position and divide it up into a number of projects or tasks that may be carried out by multiple team members. Put these abilities into a database of skills. Then you may cultivate a culture that encourages a free exchange of talent. Managers can provide initiatives that include the capabilities they're looking for. Wherever they may be, HR managers may connect projects with employees who have the required expertise. After being matched with a project, employees may discuss expectations, time commitment, etc. with the project manager. The project manager retains the power to decide who is hired for their team, whether or not they decide to employ the internal resource.

Better HR procedures will result for organisation, and decision-making bias will be eliminated. Acquiring and developing talent must be the pillars of any company if acquiring and developing talent is crucial to creating a successful one and a content workforce. The mutual trust between employer and employee may be greatly boosted through gender sensitivity, fair pay, and safety. As the designers of any company organisation, HR must periodically review its equal opportunity rules. Increasing gender diversity by placing more women in managerial roles contributes to the development of global leaders.

Assessment center technology and transition examining the future's difficulties and prospects. The crisis has been the crucial impetus for the development of technology, which has the potential to be a major facilitator by giving people the means to stay socially and emotionally linked even while physically separated. And the crisis was the catalyst for this critical shift. Talent physically left the building at the start of this crisis, and we are now starting to recognise that it is unlikely to return in many locations. Employees throughout the world have been able to continue producing even under lockdown, which will undoubtedly rank as one of the strongest examples of the incredible human potential for flexibility.

### *What are the requirements today for organisations to draw in and keep talent?*

In particular, in the present talent ecosystem where recruiters are finding it difficult to hire for new-age, in-demand talents, this chapter discusses why the ageing workforce remains as important as ever and should be viewed as a relevant talent pool in 2022. Acquired Knowledge with time senior employees can benefit from their personal and professional experiences to flourish at work. While recruiting, this is an obvious yet underutilised advantage. Senior employees can draw from their expertise during times of uncertainty since they have witnessed shifting markets, various economic situations, and personal and professional obstacles. Senior employees contribute life experiences and acquire expertise from years of employment. These assets may be used by businesses to find solutions to problems at work and to seize commercial opportunities. These employees have a wealth of accumulated expertise from working in many industries throughout the years, which aids businesses in making more informed decisions. Senior personnel also bring with them extensive and deep networks that are impossible to recreate quickly.

Although we are aware that recruiting decisions are influenced by people, automated screening technologies are also problematic. Due to their dependence on data, artificial intelligence and machine learning are often thought of as being objective. Nevertheless, an algorithm is only as objective as the data that was used to train it.Although the data is very recent, we have long-standing skill shortages. Numerous studies have been conducted on "talent shortages." Even when unemployment was high during the crisis of 2008, businesses continued to claim they couldn't find qualified employees. The constant lack of talent is a result of a gap between how quickly professions are changing and how quickly people can learn and grow.

*"In this situation, HR must adopt a far less rigid stance when addressing the issues of workflow management, process execution, and the crucial issue of flexibility."*

Analytics are being used more and more in human resources activities, from application monitoring through onboarding, retention, and data-driven decision making. Software for human capital management (HCM) may help even small firms record, collect, and publish the data necessary to increase efficiency. Accessible from anywhere and able to interface with other essential company platforms like accounting software, powerful cloud-based HCM software is available. Additionally, HCM solutions come with tools that make it simpler for your team to concentrate on long-term goals.ss of where or how they work.

With the assistance of HCM apps, you make it simpler for employees to get vital information. Additionally, your business becomes more effective by accelerating and streamlining time-consuming procedures like recruiting, time-off requests, promotions, and even job changes. This frees up time for staff to concentrate on other tasks. You may identify problem areas and develop plans of action to solve problems like high staff turnover or slow recruiting times using advanced tools.

Some of the following characteristics are to look out for:

- Approval of new hiring requisitions.
- Automating requests for leave.
- Planning and budgeting.
- Linkages to applicant tracking systems.
- Monitoring of employee records globally.
- Government identification documents and credentials.
- Onboarding processes.
- Access to real-time data.
- Built-in reporting and a dashboard.
- Recognise excellence.
- Create employee wellness programmes that are affordable or free.
- Consider strategies to increase the freedom and adaptability of employees.
- Make cross-training and career growth a priority.
- Create a day off for employees or a celebration for reaching important performance targets.

A platform that offers complete data visibility of your employees and how their skill sets and performance contribute to the success and profitability of your projects is necessary for managing employees in operational settings that are becoming more fluid. It must provide your teams with the freedom they require to create processes that work for everyone in your business.

> *"Encouragement of an age-diverse workplace has several advantages, including enhanced problem-solving, new ideas, fresh views, and knowledge-sharing. Senior employees are equally as important as younger employees, and they, too, are the workforce's future."*

Retraining techniques should be used to reimagine and leverage future talent models. Reserve your spot for the event by registering here. Talent management teams can hire better, train quicker, and grow their staff for the future with the use of talent intelligence systems like Draup, which remove workforce issues. Through D&I inspections, this analytics-driven workforce technology locates and addresses workforce shortages and supports better-informed business choices.

### Which influences our leaders more, nature or nurture?

Is it your environment or your genes? What about your careers? Do your intrinsic abilities and experiences that we bring to a job determine how far we develop professionally, or is it a combination of both? The obvious response is that both are important. The majority of us are born with particular traits or aptitudes, but education, training, and exposure to new experiences are what allow us to maximise our skills. That is why human resources (HR) experts frequently discuss "competeencies": the complex blend of both natural and learned skills that contribute to an employee's value to their organisation.

Simply said, knowledge develops with time and may be the difference between a move that advances your organisation and one that hurts it. It is clear that older employees may have a significant positive impact on younger employees. Experienced workers frequently feel appreciated and are able to help younger, less experienced workers by acting as mentors, coaches, or subject matter experts.

Organisations in almost every sector concur that they are struggling with a leadership shortage that might potentially impede their development. Because they frequently possess better communication skills than their younger colleagues, seasoned employees make wise leaders. They were raised in an era when email and instant messaging took over communication; they were familiar with how to deal with people personally. moral and dedicated to business. The satisfaction levels of senior employees help with retention, which is a major problem for businesses.

> *"The talent wars are still heated. The barriers to changing employment have been lowered for several groups of employees. Leaders may need to completely overhaul their talent strategy, reevaluating pay and benefits while also taking into account additional employee demands, including psychological safety, flexibility in scheduling and staffing, and mental and physical well-being."*

By 2026, job market will require many more tech workers to keep up with demand. At a time when having a solid technological foundation is essential for success in the digital age, there is a severe tech skills shortage facing businesses globally. In order to solve the problem, leaders must take a multifaceted approach. For example, they should establish a dedicated team to manage the entire candidate experience, provide cutting-edge planning and development tools, and foster an environment where developers and engineers are treated as creative thinkers and active participants in the process. Additionally, technology will hasten employee ownership in creation and feedback.

The following are some of the key trends that this year's senior leadership, managers, and human resources departments should take into account.

- By 2030, a billion jobs—or about one-third of the global workforce—will have undergone significant change as a result of factors like automation and artificial intelligence. Retraining and education are beneficial for both your employees and your company.
- Employees may take advantage of training opportunities and prevent burnout with the aid of promotions and transfers.
- The interactions and observations that employees have while working for a company make up the employee experience. In essence, it describes how a worker feels about their employer. It begins with the initial point of contact throughout the recruiting process, continues through onboarding, and concludes with offboarding and departure interviews. It covers everything, from interpersonal interactions to actual locations and business culture.
- HCM software may considerably assist you in enhancing the employee experience through activities including outlining career pathways, enhancing onboarding, requesting employee input, and monitoring surveys and evaluations.

- Employee engagement goes beyond the experience and examines how you may collaborate with staff to match their objectives with desired company results.

- For millions, working from home is here to stay. Employee retention and motivation when they work remotely face new difficulties. Additionally, some employers assert that it is harder to create and preserve a business culture.

- Your plans for how to manage a workforce where some workers work remotely and some cannot, such as file sharing, communication tools, and time management software, can benefit from new collaboration tools and methods.

- HCM software is more important than ever since it helps with each of these activities, making them simpler to manage and report, giving employees access to a user-friendly interface, and enabling them to operate more productively from distant locations.

- Can your team imagine itself utilising statistics to assemble the greatest roster for your company in a setting similar to "Moneyball"? A notable illustration of evidence-based talent management is the procedure shown in the hit movie "Moneyball." Decisions based on intuition and prior experience are less successful than those based on evidence.

- Getting individuals into the correct positions and swiftly deploying them is the first step in making the talent management procedure more agile. You need to communicate clearly and succinctly to achieve this properly. Instead of relying just on quarterly or annual assessments, take into account an iterative approach to assessing talent requirements and continuously gather and evaluate input from and about employees.

- Data to support evidence-based choices may be integrated into a single cloud-based solution using HCM software, particularly systems that interact with other business solutions like accounting and payroll platforms. It can support your strategic decision-making by saving and tracking yearly evaluations and other crucial financial figures.
- Flexibility The key to solving the problem is making employees feel cared about. Most organisations tend to avoid discussing employee well-being, yet it must be dealt with as effectively as possible. Flexibility is one of the top job requirements sought by senior employees. It is clear that senior employees often have obligations outside of work, such as those to their families. As they approach and pass the traditional retirement age, they could also be looking for a true work-life balance to handle the various facets of life.
- Provide innovative payment options. Allow for a range of notice durations. It helps create engaging emotional, artistic, and intellectual activities. Offer chances for physical and emotional counselling to senior ng to senior employe
- Retraining is another strategy to equip senior personnel for the future, in addition to employing them and making use of their current talents. Businesses have a challenge educating their senior personnel with in-demand skills needed to stay up with the shift and sustain strong economies as the nature of work evolves and certain positions quickly become outdated. This may be achieved by carefully reskilling and upskilling their personnel through efficient programmes.
- It pays to retain senior employees since they are accustomed to their roles and are less inclined to leave

quickly. Even though there is a large influx of younger talent, it is insufficient to replace departing senior talent, making it crucial to keep them around.

- Benefits should reflect employee values. Accept flexibility, give flexible leave policies, create opportunities for training and professional development, and honour achievements. Talk to your staff and establish connections since they regularly rate face-to-face contact as the most effective method of communication.
- Being flexible may benefit both firms and workers. Redesigning personnel management techniques should begin with recruiting the best applicants and providing recruiters with the tools they need to screen them.
- Think about how to modify your performance management, training, and remote onboarding programmes. HCM software is more important than ever since it helps with each of these activities, making them simpler to manage and report, giving employees access to a user-friendly interface, and enabling them to operate more productively from distant locations. To do this, HR directors themselves must become deeply knowledgeable in HR technology and understand how to apply technology to their organisations.

*"Senior employees are seasoned veterans who have faced a variety of difficulties over their years of employment and have refined their work ethics."*

A worker can always benefit from the nurturing that enables them to gain new skills and acquire new information, even though the essential qualities of their nature are unlikely to alter greatly over time. Therefore, talent management should focus on assisting staff members in developing and broadening their capabilities so they can perform at the greatest level possible and align their knowledge and expertise with the company's overarching goals. In other words, savvy businesses don't let their talent pool dry up. Through the whole employment lifespan, they continue to nurture it. HR specialists at these companies continue to interact with workers even after the hiring and onboarding procedures are over to evaluate their skills, take into account their goals, offer training and new opportunities, and most importantly, keep them going ahead.

> *"Talent development is just as crucial for small and medium-sized businesses as it is for giant corporations. Since talent is a scarce resource in workforces of all sizes, ignoring talent carries the same dangers as doing so: poor motivation, low productivity, and high employee turnover."*

Talent strategy intends to create a workforce of high achievers regardless of their aptitude or aspirations, but it will also assist HR experts in spotting and advancing those people who truly stand out as potential future leaders. After all, it serves no use to describe any person as "talented" if you don't provide them with the resources they require to succeed. HR can guarantee that the company they work for is developing the leaders it will need in the future by fostering their skills.

According to the 2019 Deloitte Global Human Capital Trends report, "an alternative workforce" is crucial. Less than 30% of poll participants are prepared to deal with it, despite the fact that 41% of respondents think it is a serious issue. More than half of respondents (54%) had erratic or nonexistent systems for managing such a workforce, according to the statistics.

According to Deloitte, firms that implement recognition see an increase in employee productivity, performance, and engagement of 14%. employee morale would rise and they would feel more involved in the operations of the company if they were recognised and given incentives at work. Their productivity would increase as a result of this recognition, and employers would profit from a more welcoming and productive workplace. Invest in a career in training. Training is one of the strongest strategies for keeping staff. Many businesses offer resources to their staff members so they can develop their talents. The practise of upskilling and reskilling employees should be made commonplace since it enables them to expand their skill set and discover new ways to produce high-quality outputs while maintaining their engagement and satisfaction with their professional advancement. It is far less expensive to invest in an existing employee than to go through the complete hiring process for new personnel with the required capabilities.

*"Corporate change is being driven by hybrid work. Since the widespread availability of computers, the concept of a location-agnostic workforce has gained popularity, although it wasn't considered an immediate possibility until 2020. This was partially caused by organisational inertia since both our customers' and partners' systems, procedures, and workflows were focused on the office."*

The fact that organisations had a natural predisposition to take an "all or nothing" attitude toward flexibility until relatively recently also had a role in this. The previous categorical rejection of flexible or hybrid work was founded on very valid issues, although unpopular with many. The addition of several new working methods would have undoubtedly exacerbated operational complexity, which is increasing year after year. Due to the forced adoption of remote and hybrid working during the past two years, enterprises have had to refocus their digital transformation initiatives on supporting hybrid working. Adopting the tools and technology to facilitate alterations in workplace dynamics, It has historically been reactive and heavily reliant on financial results to adopt new HR toolkits and technologies. However, significant changes in how we perceive work are pushing HR technology to the fore.

The level playing field that most groups desire is made possible by technology as businesses try to increase diversity, equity, and inclusion. Formal coaching has always been viewed as an executive perk, either provided to strong performers to keep them satisfied or to sharpen their leadership abilities. Companies miss out on a significant development tool that may offer young leaders individualised development before they form habits that need to be unlearned as a result of this haphazard approach.

> *"The introduction of automated coaching technologies and digital platforms is changing that value proposition and opening up the possibility of mass coaching."*

According to the Sapient Insights Group 2020–2021 HR Systems Survey, traditional ways of people management are losing ground while non-traditional approaches are rising in popularity (gated behind form). 15% of businesses expect to spend less on traditional HR technology in 2021, on average by 23% less than their present budgets. 28% of businesses want to spend more on non-traditional HR expenses like infrastructure and tools for remote workers. More than 30% of businesses are reviewing their hiring, learning, and scheduling methods.By 2025, the LMS market is anticipated to be valued at $28.1 billion, based on the most recent market data by Meticulous Research. Empathy is a crucial component of intelligent and comprehensive personnel management. It is baked into many of the other trends in talent management, such as employee experience and highlighting talents.

Businesses spend a lot of time and money interviewing, hiring, and training new hires only to have them quit after a short while. In a poll conducted in 2019, approximately 6 out of 10 participants named work ethic as one of the key distinctions between the young and old. 90% of the respondents with experience felt that having an "ethical" workplace is "very or very vital." According to the 2019 SHRM Global Skills Shortage Study, more than half of respondents believe that the situation has "worsened or considerably worsened" during the last two years. More than half of the 600+ respondents to a recent poll by Wiley Education Services said their firm has talent shortages. In addition, the same survey discovered that 57% of participants ranked upskilling and/or reskilling as their preferred option for closing the skills gap. According to the SHRM research, companies have a variety of alternatives for addressing the skills gap. Increasing training efforts, using the contingent workforce, and putting policies in place that support employee retention are some of the strategies.

Skills gap of problem-solving and resiliency, it has usefullness senior employees may assist in resolving a range of issues that may develop at work, including complicated business choices or workplace disagreements, thanks to their expertise, maturity, and soothing impact. They have developed the ability to think critically, which can assist them in making judgments without guidance or second guessing.

> "*Senior employees are frequently more resilient when presented with a company's difficulties since they have typically encountered challenging periods throughout their working lives. This links directly to their leadership abilities and makes them powerful enough to support their company when things go wrong.*"

What options do organisations have? Recognizing the necessity and advantages of having an age-diverse workforce is a terrific starting step, but the true problem is being able to recruit and keep older personnel. Let's talk about recruiting and keeping experienced personnel to make use of this skill pool.

From a larger perspective, HR technology is essential to maintaining competitiveness. According to a Gartner poll, two out of every three corporate executives believe that their organisations must adopt technology if they don't want to become obsolete. The talent management environment is ever-evolving. To keep up with developments in both the digital and human domains, businesses must adapt TM.

A few years ago, when AI first appeared on the scene, there was a fear that robots might take human jobs. But it turns out that the concern was exaggerated. Instead, AI should be seen as enhancing human employees rather than taking their place. While some jobs may be lost, in my opinion, many more are changing, according to the Deloitte assessment.

It's obvious that AI is something that businesses should be interested in acquiring. The good news is that most LMS systems now include AI integrations, which makes it even simpler to benefit from its technical advantages. It's not simple to reskill and close the skill gap, but that doesn't imply it has to be any harder. To close the skills gap and address reskilling, businesses can employ LMS software, learning experience platforms (LXPs), and other solutions. These systems can offer micro-learning, which provides users with instant access to little bits of knowledge like videos and articles. They also provide macro-learning, which allows users to go deeper into a subject, MOOCs (massive open online courses), or other methods of distribution that assist in the development of new abilities.

### *How and where will AI improve talent management going ahead in 2022?*

Although the AI tendency is nothing new, anticipated it will be taking centre stage. As AI develops based on "learning" experiences, we will observe how it streamlines the hiring and onboarding processes. One well-known HR function where AI is having a big influence and adding considerable value is recruiting. 96% of senior HR professionals, according to Ideal, think AI has the ability to significantly improve talent attraction and retention. Another analysis from inside BIGDATA claims that chatbots on career sites increase the number of job seekers converted into leads by 95% and outperform career sites without them in terms of candidate conversion. Chatbots are used by businesses to respond to common inquiries, giving their recruitment staff more time to work with the pool of prospects.

> *"Organisations are employing AI to manage the wide range of procedures involved in hiring, in large part due to the benefits it delivers in terms of speed and automation. The necessity for personnel to oversee AI systems has grown along with their use."*

As with any cutting-edge technology, AI has some red flags attached. One problem that is frequently brought up is that, even while hiring prejudice can be addressed, AI systems could unintentionally have the programmers' bias built in. It is vital to properly investigate any AI-enabled solutions you are thinking about and search for any flaws that could jeopardise your attempts to up your talent acquisition game.

By utilising AI, the majority of organisations have switched to asking for instantaneous or continuous input. However, in order to make this feedback meaningful, it must be possible to gather personal insights that can be connected to personal growth and development.

Artificial intelligence (AI) is being used by more organisations to enhance employee experience and better interpret data collected from various employee life-cycle touchpoints. Talent acquisition is one area where organisations have made significant investments. The HR staff gathers a variety of data during the recruiting, promotion, and employee life-cycle processes. In order to improve areas like employee experience and how we evaluate and segment our people for growth, our best hope is to leverage AI to better analyse this data. Another method to make use of this is to observe future patterns of the things that your people are responding to more frequently as compared to less frequently, and then use this information to more accurately estimate the likelihood of any intervention being successful.

*"The talent management sector of the HR market, in particular, is going through a significant transition. Everything is in motion, from the development of AI to the challenges posed by talent and the skills gap. It takes work to implement efficient talent management procedures."*

Despite the worries, there are more advantages to AI than drawbacks. Companies should consider using AI-enabled personnel management tools to speed up the hiring process, increase hiring quality, and save expenses. The way businesses are run has undergone a metamorphosis during the past two years. Worldwide industries were affected by the COVID-19 epidemic, which significantly changed how most organisations did business. The majority of workforces were shifted to remote locations overnight, establishing a new reality and making technology essential for maintaining businesses. The market has plenty of promise, nevertheless, at the same time. There is an astonishing amount of innovation, enabling businesses to address certain issues like hiring prejudice and a lack of diversity in the workplace. Organisations that implement these changes and continue to innovate in their human resource management strategies will be better positioned for long-term success.And choosing the proper software is the first step in that procedure.

When traditional organisational structures give way to more flexible cross-functional teams, you may make use of AI in other ways, such as:

- Imagine receiving continuous, immediate feedback on every engagement you have at work.
- Most organisations have shifted to asking for immediate or ongoing input. To make this feedback effective, though, it would be necessary to be able to gather personal insights that can be connected to growth and development.
- The capacity to design tailored career paths based on aptitudes, potential, and prospective future jobs of interest.
- The future is in providing a roadmap for people to progress vertically, horizontally, or diagonally inside an organisation depending on their professional aspirations (what skills to learn, where to acquire them from, linking workers to mentors or coaches, etc.).
- Every firm will prioritise reskilling as the digital skills gap widens. Core digital abilities will soon be just as crucial as reading and writing.

In the future, it will be commonplace to work remotely or in a hybrid capacity, and it will be crucial to prioritise employee digital engagement. Businesses are speeding innovation to create smarter, safer, more resilient organisations that prioritise the employee experience. Greater flexibility and balance for employees are made possible by the hybrid model, which combines remote work and in-office experiences. Workflows will be the gasoline that enables organisations to speed up employee experiences as we enter a new year. Employees will place a high value on organisations that provide meaningful work, chances to make an impact, and cultures that promote wellbeing as they reexamine what it means to be an employee in general. The ability to provide employees the flexibility, autonomy, and choice of where they work, when they work, and how they work is what workflow will enable organisations to do.

The most important stakeholders for firms will be their employees. Because of the epidemic, organisations are now putting their people first at a level that was previously unheard of. Additionally, organisations that foster stronger employee engagement and dedication will have much faster top-line growth rates. The already severe skills gap will worsen, and retraining will take on more importance. Because there aren't enough employees with the necessary set of digital skills, businesses are confronting a new issue in a world that is increasingly dominated by digital technology. Emerging technologies like Artificial Intelligence (AI) and Machine Learning (ML) are largely to blame for the gap's continued widening since they are intensifying the need for digital capabilities.

*"Every organisation will prioritise reskilling as the digital skills gap widens. Core digital abilities will soon be just as crucial as reading and writing. Businesses will need to address the need for training, reskilling, and providing employees with the tools they need to do the jobs that the economy's digital transformation demands."*

If HR professionals do not leverage data and analytics to develop insights into organisational health, they will fall behind. Traditional HR's heyday has long since passed. Even when the job descriptions or duties have not yet changed, it is crucial to begin adjusting to the new reality. You need to start by honing your talents in the crucial areas that experts believe are essential for future professional success and are expected to be extensively used. They consist of business strategy, analytics, and people, naturally.

There are now many solutions accessible for working remotely, but soon there will be more improvements. Technology like Artificial Intelligence (AI), Machine Learning (ML), Data Analytics, and the Cloud are being used by talent managers and leaders in their talent management ecosystem at an increasing rate. With AI-based sourcing, assessment, screening, interviewing, and applicant experience management, recruiting is a significant AI market in HR. To improve recruiting, HR directors are using data, clever algorithms, and social sensing technologies. A crucial component of personnel management is skill development and reskilling. Establishing training and reskilling routes is crucial to assisting individuals in moving into new or upgraded professions. Augmented reality (AR) and virtual reality (VR) will be used more to integrate a successful system and quicken staff training and development.

The requirement for reskilling owing to shifting employment requirements is another element at play. According to the 2019 Deloitte Human Capital Trends report, 54% of respondents said their company will increase spending on "workforce reskilling" somewhat or significantly. Organisations nowadays must use cutting-edge technologies to stay up with the changing nature of the labour force while keeping reskilling in mind. As a result, AI technology has emerged as one of the most useful resources in the talent management sector. 54% of CEOs, claim that using AI at work has enhanced productivity. The workplace will be more shaped by millennials and Gen Z as the baby boomer generation continues to retire. Additionally, job change is the norm for both generations, whether or not businesses want it. One in four workers, including 33% of Gen Z and 25% of millennials, expects to change careers, according to research by IBM's Institute of Business Value.

Agility will be essential in this new era to help firms combat the propensity for job hopping. That includes making investments in software programmes that lower the cost of onboarding and training new employees. Companies must also create an environment that attracts new employees rather than repels them. Productivity is declining despite full employment. The difficulty with TM is determining whether the answer rests in technology, older methods, or a combination of both. Although always beneficial, engagement surveys and pulse checks are definitely no replacement for a genuine connection built on respect, acknowledgement, and trust. A Gartner study reveals that stability, pay, and work-life balance are the top methods to recruit workers for businesses trying to retain their talent. Thanks to artificial intelligence (AI), periodic pulse checks, questionnaires, and psychometric analysis may now be simply integrated into online and mobile chatbots and made available to employees.

Today's job searchers and employees demand more than just two weeks of vacation time and job happiness. They desire a great professional experience at every stage, from the hiring process through their position within the organisation. Before we explore a world where technology and humans coexist, it's wise to get a comprehensive understanding of the market. Being flexible may benefit both firms and workers. Redesigning personnel management techniques should begin with recruiting the best applicants and providing recruiters with the tools they need to screen them. Think about how to modify your performance management, training, and remote onboarding programmes.

### *What recommendations do I have for integrating people analytics into the business, not simply HR?*

With people analytics teams in most large organisations, advanced analytics is revolutionising the HR sector. The HR Technology Market 2021 research by Josh Bersin paints a less optimistic outlook. Only 16% of businesses, according to the report, have a plan for handling gig labour, and only 12% of them were judged to be strong performers in this regard. Even while some systems provide the required capabilities, the market is relatively young. However, I believe that the market for vendors is primed for substantial growth as a result of the rising need for solutions that make managing a contingent workforce easier. To effectively traverse the world of new items while your firm searches for solutions in this developing industry, it will be crucial to comprehend your requirements and carry out an in-depth study.

> *"Companies must rethink talent management and the tools used to implement it in light of the current work environment and the number of freelancers and contractors."*

Instead of focusing simply on the "here and now," any type of people analytics needs to be tightly integrated with broader company objectives and culture across short-, mid-, and long-term goals. In 2022, how do you think businesses will use people analytics to address issues like The Great Resignation while improving employee satisfaction?

Assessing the business impact of turnover is crucial as we examine the employee life cycle. You normally analyse the data to find the factors that increase the danger of flight in order to aid retention. While there may be a variety of reasons for leaving a job, we increasingly see the emphasis on "remain" decisions changing toward actual employee experiences, which are influenced by culture and ultimately serve as the major difference. Utilising analytics to offer clear human insights on why people don't engage and quit helps us to intervene where it matters most, establish a culture that supports a "sticky quotient," and manage retention as an organisation works to create a 100-year success narrative.

Employees are not only temporary solutions for getting talent; they are in it for the long haul. When a candidate is acquired rather than recruited, you must take everything into account, including abilities, potential development, and cultural fit. Finding, finding, and employing quality personnel has grown to be quite difficult in the present job market. Most corporate executives place a high focus on talent acquisition. Therefore, it shouldn't come as a surprise to anybody if businesses outperform their rivals to get top people in a market that is more candidate-driven.

The substance of the "people" underlying the data should not be lost in the process of people analytics, which is a crucial point to convey. Because humans are complicated creatures that function in social and organisational contexts, it is crucial to discover these social networks and the major influences that exist inside them using relational analytics. Everything you do in this area right now is meant to improve company value, people's experiences, and our capacity to gauge effect. There is every reason for organisations to adopt people analytics given its significance in knowing not just how the business operates but also getting to the fundamental cause of why a business performs in the manner it does.

Looking beyond hiring, 83% of HR leaders recognise the importance of a great customer experience to a business's success. Because of this, businesses need to develop a positive workplace culture where workers feel empowered and can be effective. A variety of instruments, such as performance management and succession planning, are offered to achieve that aim. Look for software that offers features like annual performance evaluations, survey-based feedback, reporting tools to monitor progress, and other features.

In order to meet the talent demands of the future, HRM will have to rethink its employee engagement and performance management practises. Redesigning personnel management for globally distributed and contingent workforces would require a far greater level of personalisation than was previously possible thanks to AI and other types of technology. It's hardly surprising that businesses are prioritising applicant experience this year, particularly in recruiting. Great candidate experience grew from 25% to 31% during 2019, according to the 2020 Talent Board Research Report.

Talent Analytics Make the agility that is required for agility companies that use a comprehensive talent model today use business KPIs in addition to labour data to inform decision-making. And AI will be essential for drawing out useful insights from the information and data being received. People analytics may also assist firms in making more sensible business decisions. Organisations should take into account the data sources that might alter access to, competition for, and the applicability of skill sets before implementing analytics to optimise their workforce. To reduce costs and the time it takes to fill positions, organisations can use market data at the job level.

*"Talent acquisition and contingent workforce data may provide hiring managers with greater insight into the possibilities available to fill a post, in addition to data on the current resources."*

A well-known trend is augmented analytics, a data-driven technique that automates insights using language processing and machine learning. Employee data is evaluated and analysed by augmented analytics to produce more insightful results, identify patterns, and monitor important metrics. The information is then delivered in an approachable, conversational way. It is uncommon for businesses to immediately locate the top candidates for their available positions. Most HR managers have long sought to improve DE&I (Diversity, Equity, and Inclusion). According to the SHL-Lighthouse analysis, businesses with the greatest results (revenue, staff retention) are more likely to assemble a broad group of stakeholders to support talent mobility efforts. Organisations must use internal recruitment to fill crucial positions and skill gaps. Because it empowers them, fosters their growth, and builds their faith in the company, internal candidates perform better in their jobs. According to a joint survey by SHL and

Lighthouse, 88% of employees would stay at a job longer if there were possibilities for professional growth.

Candidates that pass the job-filtering process will be chosen based on criteria including location, knowledge, skills, and abilities (KSAs), or demographic data. HR specialists may learn more about candidate behaviour by analysing the data from career centres. By doing this, businesses would be able to use that data to build pipelines that are specific to both current employees and potential new hires. Think about whether your system needs to be upgraded or if there are any extra features that might help you produce these experiences.

Global market data may help organisations determine where to set up shop to access the best talent pools at the line-business level. Finally, analytics can offer a long-term roadmap of the talents that are now available within the workforce of a business. According to a recent survey report, 42% of companies indicate they are increasing their spending on predictive people analytics, while 36% say they are maintaining their budgets in this area.

> *"There is a give-and-take dynamic in the connection between an employer and employee. Every talent wants to be recognised for their contributions to the organisation's expansion. Employers must take cautious action to make sure they keep up with the labour ecosystem's constant evolution and provide the best possible working environment for their employees."*

The most secure TM strategy to achieve is to take cautious action to make sure that the organisation develop through time, push limits, and present deals with distinctive advantages that nobody else will. Organisations need to establish a culture that encourages collaboration and maximises the effects of creativity and innovation. These elements may assist firms greatly in recruiting and keeping their talent in the midst of the "War for Talent", when every company wants to work with the greatest talent available. These elements have the power to change the recruiting game and demonstrate to businesses how to approach contemporary hiring with empathy and openness. They are essential to the company's future development and will eventually help them prevail in the talent competition.

### *How much time have you spent contemplating the talent operations strategy for your business?*

Most likely, not much longer than it took you to read it. Whether you realise it or not, all businesses have an operational model for their talent. This model serves as the framework for all of your organisation's talents and capabilities, just like the operating system does for a digital device. Most businesses still use a hierarchical management structure with command-and-control systems as their main operational paradigm. In this paradigm, employees are employed to do predetermined tasks that include a job description and a list of required competencies. Only abilities that are pertinent to a job description are often of interest to a corporation. Anything beyond that is seen as irrelevant. Functional managers often oversee staff members in this talent-based operational style. Typically, a new hire's career path is restricted to the sub-functional silo to which they are initially assigned. The majority of businesses still operate according to this conventional, hierarchical talent operational paradigm, despite all the rhetoric of flatter organisations and dismantling functional silos.

*"In order to change the model, several organisations use matrixed, cross-functional project teams. But the majority of employees go up the functional ladder, and the most crucial choices are still made in a top-down fashion."*

Despite the limitless opportunities that digitisation offers, far too many individuals are still working constantly at their maximum capacity and scarcely have time for all of their interests and desires that are still unmet. The 40-hour workweek has run its course. With less but wiser, more cooperative labour, many objectives may be accomplished. However, only if the ongoing interaction with several teams does not become a chore in and of itself. Companies must teach staff to utilise digital technologies and to communicate with one another, for instance, when it comes to providing positive feedback or declining requests from coworkers. Because of the resulting freedom, we will be much closer to the original vision of "New Employment," in which paid work takes a back seat to what individuals truly genuinely desire.

Depending on its size, vision, goals, and a variety of other elements, every organisation has a unique approach to culture. Any organisation should establish its culture using a four-pronged "People First" strategy. Everything starts at home, just like charity. How you treat your family will show in how you handle employees. In every important decision, including hiring, talent is always prioritised over antiquated customs like hierarchy. The team's well-being is taken care of in all respects, with special attention paid to physical, mental, and intellectual health.

A great vision is useless without excellent people. in Jim Collins' book, "Good to Great. This quotation demonstrates the significance of employing and developing staff members in order to build a talent pool and accomplish the exponential development for your corporation that the company's founders had envisioned. The most crucial human resource activity is hiring, which is followed by strong onboarding procedures, practical and efficient training, and coaching sessions that increase productivity throughout any firm. Therefore, once people become a high-value resource for your business, you can rely on them to make a fantastic concept a reality.

Organisations are reevaluating their business strategies to preserve a competitive edge in the future in a fast expanding "linear" environment. To achieve this, organisations must be steered toward a highly trained labour pool that comprises specialised individuals in order to fulfil their changing business objectives. This is why the journey to acquire a future-ready workforce is a crucial strategic step. When it comes to employing a workforce that is future-ready, it is advisable to first comprehend the changing organisational demands, which may be discovered through current employment trends. In this respect, the upGrad Career Report 2021 indicates that the technology vertical, which rose by 30% to 42% in the second quarter of 2021, is leading the increase in hiring throughout the Indian labour market, closely followed by data analytics, which climbed by 22% to 37%. This trend indicates that the best candidates in the nation's job market have next-generation IT skills. But this talent search is more complicated than it seems.

The management's first priority will be the rationalisation of the workforce. During the epidemic, there have been a lot of layoffs, with performers and underperformers taking the brunt of the action.

Organisations will be reducing expenses while building a successful runway with their most valuable and productive workers. Employers will benefit from the epidemic by eliminating underperformers. Employee experience will become a bigger priority in talent management following the pandemic. Employers will need to develop strategies to improve superior employee experience across the board in the HR department as there will be fewer people available and the same amount of work to be done. In the post-pandemic period, performance management, which was formerly an annual phenomenon, will be targeted and short-term.

According to a survey report report, 73% of CEOs believe that HR technology helps their talent teams better focus on tasks that are important to the business. Additionally, 70% of respondents say that AI will create new opportunities for businesses like theirs. Additionally, almost 71% believe that AI and robotics will improve recruiting practises. About 71% of respondents think they can find, entice, and work with more qualified individuals. While 52% think that widespread use of AI would result in employment losses, 72% think that it will actually create new work opportunities. Process engineers will need to focus more on the continuous division of labour between machines and people in such a situation. Organisations will also need to think about how much more valuable humans are in certain roles than a machine.

It is only logical to believe that the digital giants have access to a sizable majority of the top tech talent on the market given the rapid digitisation of corporate processes and the high demand for skills like Cloud Architecture, Cybersecurity, Full Stack Development, and AI/ML. However, this does not imply that startups, unicorns, or other non-tech companies are not searching for qualified IT people. The top industries recruiting for analytics are banking and financial services, energy and utilities, and media and entertainment, in that order. This raises the question of how these industries can compete with IT powerhouses for top employees, as well as where they will get candidates with the necessary skills.

Businesses nowadays are searching for more efficient ways to leverage technology to enhance their goods, services, and operations. Because they can write specialised code, are knowledgeable about and highly skilled in most aspects of web and application development, and can write specialised code, full-stack developers are needed in the capital markets where businesses take on large or specialised projects in investment banking, asset servicing, and cyber security. As the distinction between front-end and back-end becomes increasingly hazy, more developers are becoming full-stack developers. According to the US Bureau of Labor Statistics, by 2024 there will be 8,533,000 openings for full-stack developers. As a result of organisations' strong focus on lowering resource costs, this role will provide workers with a wide range of employment opportunities.

Data analysts are highly sought after not just in India but all throughout the world. Data analysts must be hired since users are more eager than ever to contribute their information. Finding and analysing the data needed to launch and expand a firm are the duties of a data analyst. In the past, only industry giants like Amazon, Google, Facebook, and financial institutions would flaunt the data of their actual and future consumers, but now, every company understands the value of leveraging consumer data to improve its goods and services. As a consequence, one may now prepare for a future career as a data analyst in India.

Finally, I consider HR to be a counsellor to both the business and the employee in today's workplace. They serve as a link between the two and are crucial to the organisation's growth and change. I think the last 24 months of the epidemic have taught us some crucial lessons. In order to accomplish the results they are accountable for delivering, leaders are now required to provide some level of choice and empowerment over how, when, and where their teams and individuals work. Continuous periods of experimentation, trial-and-error, adaptation, and agility will be necessary for this. Inflexible and restrictive approaches that are being reintroduced only because they were successful "pre-pandemic" face a significant danger of alienating people and failing to meet their present requirements, values, and expectations.

*"A business may recruit new applicants and keep its precious assets by fostering employee enthusiasm and designing a personalised employee development programme for each worker. An organisation will see improved accountability, efficiency, and leadership drive from its employees if it regularly acknowledges and rewards their contributions." - Dr. Amit Das*

# About The Author

*Dr. Amit Das, is a renowned executive advisor, consultant, educationist, author, speaker and coach whose 25+ years of business experience provides high-impact, practical solutions that support his clients' leadership development and organisational transformations. Dr. Amit Das is recognised as an innovative, principled thought leader who combines intellectual rigor and discipline with an ability to translate theory into practice. His operational skills are coupled with a strategic ability to analyse, develop, and implement successful strategies for profitability, growth, and sustainability.*

*Dr. Amit Das has a successful track record in aligning learning and training solutions to key business strategy with a strong focus on flawless execution excellence to facilitate individual, business divisional, and organisational performance. He keeps relentless focus on measuring training impact and ROI, people capability building graphs, training process governance, performance coaching, and strategic thinking. These have been some of his key individual success traits. His core capabilities include performance coaching, designing training and development frameworks, psychometric assessment and analysis, competency framework development and assessments, content design and facilitation of soft skills and leadership programmes, Learning Management Systems, Learning Impact Measurement, Talent Analysis, and Performance Coaching and Counselling.*

*He has a Ph.D. and a Fellowship in strategic learning, along with his first class degrees in Human Resource Management, Marketing Management, International Business, and Corporate Laws from the top business schools in India. He is a certified Psychometric analyst, OD*

*Interventionist, Human Psychologist, Lifecoach, Black Belt (LSS), Strategic Thinker, Talent Analyst, professional coach from the U.K. and behavioral coach from the U.S.A.*

# References


- *Talent Management: A Practical Guide (Optimise Book 10) Kindle Editionby Sorin Dumitrascu (Author) Format: Kindle Edition, 4 Oct 2021.*
- *The Talent Pool: How to Find and Keep Dedicated People While Making a Lasting Impact Kindle Edition by Sharon Ryan (Author), Cynthia Tolsma (Author) Format: Kindle Edition*
- *The Executive Guide to Integrated Talent Management Paperback – Import, 16 June 2011 by Pat Galagan (Editor), Kevin Oakes (Editor).*
- *How To Develop An Innovation Talent Succession Plan : Tools for Creating Innovation Skills Bench-Strength in Organizations by David Masumba | 4 November 2020.*
- *Talent Mindset: The Business Owner's Guide to Building Bench Strength by Stacy Feiner | 25 February 2015.*
- *Leaders at All Levels: Deepening Your Talent Pool to Solve the Succession Crisis (J-B US non-Franchise Leadership) by Ram Charan | 15 January 2008.*
- *Talent Management in the Developing World: Adopting a Global Perspective by Joel Alemibola Elegbe | 10 June 2019.*
- *Off the Bench Leadership: Get Ready to Take your Shot by Jerry Busone | 1 November 2014.*
- *Rebel Talent: Why It Pays to Break the Rules at Work and in Life by Francesca Gino | 1 May 2018.*
- *Reinventing Talent Management: Principles and Practices for the New World of Work (1ˢᵗ Ed.) Audio CD – Unabridged, May 22, 2017 by Edward E. Lawler III (Author), Wayne Shepherd (Narrator).*
- *Common Sense Talent Management: Using Strategic*

Human Resources to Improve Company Performance 1ˢᵗ Edition by Steven T. Hunt (Author), Sep 2018.

- *Talent Generation: How Visionary Organizations Are Redefining Work and Achieving Greater Success Hardcover – July 31, 2017 by Sarah Sladek (Author).*
- *Talent Magnet: How to Attract and Keep the Best People: 3 (The High Performance Series) Hardcover – 27 February 2018.*
- *The Talent Manifesto: How Disrupting People Strategies Maximizes Business Results (BUSINESS BOOKS) Hardcover – Import, 19 March 2019 by RJ Heckman (Author).*
- *Bet on Talent: How to Create a Remarkable Culture That Wins the Hearts of Customers Hardcover – 3 September 2019 by Dee Ann Turner (Author), Patrick Lencioni (Foreword).*
- *Talent Force: A New Manifesto for the Human Side of Business Hardcover – 13 January 2006 by Rusty Rueff (Author), Hank Stringer (Author).*
- *The Talent Masters: Why Smart Leaders Put People Before Numbers Hardcover – Deckle Edge, 9 November 2010 by Bill Conaty (Author), Ram Charan (Author).*
- *High Potential: How to Spot, Manage and Develop Talented People at Work Kindle Edition by Ian MacRae (Author), Adrian Furnham (Author), & 1 More Format: Kindle Edition, Feb 2018.*
- *Managing Talent: Recruiting, Retaining, and Getting the Most from Talented People (Economist Books) Hardcover – 4 March 2014 by Marion Devine (Author), Michel Syrett (Author), The Economist (Author).*
- *The Leadership Pipeline: How to Build the Leadership Powered Company Hardcover – Illustrated, January 11, 2011 by Stephen Drotter (Author), Ram Charan (Author).*

James L. Noel (Author).

- *Effective Succession Planning: Ensuring Leadership Continuity and Building Talent from Within Hardcover – Import, 1 May 2010 by William J Rothwell (Author).*
- *The Talent Management Handbook: Creating a Sustainable Competitive Advantage by Selecting, Developing, and Promoting the Best People Hardcover – 1 July 2017 by Lance Berger (Author), Dorothy Berger (Author).*
- *One Page Talent Management: Eliminating Complexity, Adding Value Hardcover – 18 May 2010 by Effron (Author).*
- *Best Practices in Talent Management: How the World's Leading Corporations Manage, Develop, and Retain Top Talent (Pfeiffer Essential Resources for Training and HR Professionals (Hardcover)) Hardcover – Illustrated, 26 January 2010 by Marshall Goldsmith (Author), Louis Carter (Author), The Best Practice Institute (Author).*
- *Demystifying Talent Management: Unleash People's Potential to Deliver Superior Results Paperback – January 26, 2015 by Kimberly Janson.*
- *Talent Management, A Contemporary Perspective Edited by: Mamta Mohapatra & Swati Dhir, Aug 2021.*
- *Inclusive Talent Management: How Business can Thrive in an Age of Diversity Paperback – 3 July 2016 by Stephen Frost (Author), Danny Kalman (Author).*
- *The Oxford Handbook of Talent Management (Oxford Handbooks) 1$^{st}$ Edition by David G Collings (Editor), Kamel Mellahi (Editor), Wayne F. Cascio (Editor), Sep 2017.*
- *Strategic Talent Management, Creating the Right Workforce By Robert J. Greene, March, 2020.*
- *Effective Talent Management, Aligning Strategy, People*

*and Performance By Mark Wilcox, Dec 2020.*

- *Global Talent Management: An Integrated Approach Paperback – 29 January 2019 by Sonal Minocha (Author), Dean Hristov (Author).*
- *Reinventing Talent Management: How to Maximize Performance in the New Marketplace Hardcover – Import, 21 July 2009 by William A. Schiemann (Author), Susan R. Meisinger (Foreword).*
- *Talent on Demand: Managing Talent in the Age of Uncertainty Hardcover – 10 April 2008 by Cappelli.*
- *Aha Moments in Talent Management: A Business Fable With Practical Exercises Kindle Edition by Mark Allen (Author) Format: Kindle Edition, 22 Aug 2014.*
- *Macro Talent Management: A Global Perspective on Managing Talent in Developed Markets (Global HRM) by Vlad Vaiman, Paul Sparrow, et al. | 25 July 2018.*
- *Digitalised Talent Management: Navigating the Human-Technology Interface (Routledge Focus on Business and Management) by Sharna Wiblen | 1 February 2021.*
- *Talent Management in Small and Medium Enterprises: Context, Practices and Outcomes (Routledge Focus on Issues in Global Talent Management) by Aleksy Pocztowski, Urban Pauli, et al. | 6 May 2022.*
- *Careers and Talent Management: A Critical Perspective (Routledge Focus on Business and Management) by Cristina Reis | 7 December 2015.*
- *The Talent War: How Special Operations and Great Organizations Win on Talent by Mike Sarraille , George Randle , et al. | 10 November 2020.*
- *The Talent Code: Greatness isn't born. It's grown by Daniel Coyle | 15 October 2020.*
- *Managing to Make a Difference: How to Engage, Retain, and Develop Talent for Maximum Performance by Larry*

Sternberg and Kim Turnage | 10 April 2017.

- *Talent is Overrated 2nd Edition: What Really Separates World-Class Performers from Everybody Else* by Geoff Colvin | 7 February 2019.
- *Rebel Talent: Why it Pays to Break the Rules at Work and in Life* by Francesca Gino | 7 February 2019.
- *Employer Branding for Competitive Advantage: Models and Implementation Strategies (Information Technology, Management and Operations Research Practices)* by Geeta Rana, Shivani Agarwal, et al. | 22 March 2021.
- *Talent is Overrated: What Really Separates World-Class Performers from Everybody Else* by Geoff Colvin | 11 January 2011.
- *Keeping the People Who Keep you in Business: 24 Ways to Hang On to Your Most Valuable Talent* by BRANHAM | 16 December 2000.
- *Beyond Talent: Become Someone Who Gets Extraordinary Results* by John C. Maxwell | 18 April 2011.
- *Global Talent Management: Challenges, Strategies, and Opportunities (Management for Professionals)* by Akram Al Ariss | 3 September 2016.
- *Superbosses: How Exceptional Leaders Master the Flow of Talent* by Sydney Finkelstein | 8 March 2017.
- *Wingspan: Talent Management - Gaining Corporate Dominance* by Adrienne Somerville | 28 February 2021.
- *Talent Management Agenda in a Post Covid-19 World: A Practical Talent and Succession Management Guide for Professionals, Executives and Business Leaders.* by Adebayo Akinloye | 29 May 2020.
- *Righteous Recruiting: Essays on Reinventing Talent Acquisition for People* by Elizabeth Ryan | 29 July 2020.
- *Talent Management in Latin America: Pressing Issues and Best Practices (Routledge Focus on Issues in Global Talent*

*Management) by Jordi Trullen and Jaime Bonache | 9 May 2021.*

- *The Talent Era: Achieving a High Return on Talent (Financial Times (Prentice Hall)) by Subir Chowdhury | 17 December 2001.*
- *Integrated Talent Management Scorecards: Insights From World-Class Organizations on Demonstrating Value by Toni Hodges DeTuncq and Lynn Schmidt | 13 January 2014.*
- *Talent Doesn't Grow on Trees: How to Hire Your Next Superstar by Angelo Giallombardo | 7 April 2022.*
- *Talent Management Technologies: A Buyer's Guide to New, Innovative Solutions by Allan Schweyer, Ed Newman, et al. | 16 July 2009.*